SUNDAY COMES EVERY WEEK

Sunday Comes Every Week

Daily Habits for the Busy Preacher

Frank G. Honeycutt

WILLIAM B. EERDMANS PUBLISHING COMPANY
GRAND RAPIDS, MICHIGAN

Wm. B. Eerdmans Publishing Co.
4035 Park East Court SE, Grand Rapids, Michigan 49546
www.eerdmans.com

25 24 23 22 21 20 19   1 2 3 4 5 6 7

ISBN 978-0-8028-7645-4

Library of Congress Cataloging-in-Publication Data

Names: Honeycutt, Frank G., 1957– author.
Title: Sunday comes every week : daily habits for the busy preacher /
    Frank G. Honeycutt.
Description: Grand Rapids, Michigan : William B. Eerdmans Publishing
    Company, 2019. | Includes bibliographical references.
Identifiers: LCCN 2018056244 | ISBN 9780802876454 (pbk. : alk. paper)
Subjects: LCSH: Preaching. | Pastoral theology.
Classification: LCC BV4211.3 .H665 2019 | DDC 251—dc23
    LC record available at https://lccn.loc.gov/2018056244

Contents

Foreword
by Thomas G. Long   vii

Introduction   1

1. **MONDAY**   10
   Listening

2. **TUESDAY**   21
   Hearing

3. **WEDNESDAY**   41
   Exegeting

4. **THURSDAY**   63
   Naming

5. **REFLECTING**   87
   A Pastor Looks Back

CONTENTS

6. **FRIDAY**   104
   Writing

7. **SATURDAY**   127
   Rehearsing

8. **SUNDAY**   131
   Offering

   Epilogue   143

   Notes   145

   Bibliography   153

Foreword

Frank Honeycutt has—and we can all be grateful for this—pastoral imagination. The term "pastoral imagination" was coined by Craig Dykstra, who in his many years heading up the religion division of the Lilly Endowment was fascinated by what made ministers tick. He was particularly intrigued by the way that some pastors, like some lawyers, physicians, artists, and novelists, rise above the average to a level of extraordinary and stunning excellence in the practice of their vocation. He wondered how such excellence, which was a great gift to the church, could be spotted in advance, educated, cultivated, and nourished. He concluded that a few pastors, certainly not all and not even most, simply bring a wealth of talent and a willingness to learn to the long path of ministry, allowing them to develop "a way of seeing in depth and of creating new realities." He writes,

> Such ministry has about it a freshness, an improvisatory character, a liveliness that is itself infectious. Thus an imagination that is at its heart a seeing in depth—seeing reality

truthfully—turns out to be an imagination full of creativity, an imagination that sees what is not yet and begins to create it.[1]

We see this vitality and faithful innovation in these pages as Frank Honeycutt draws wisdom from his many years of parish ministry. The first evidence of his pastoral imagination is the way he tells stories. These are no stylized tales of success with the triumphant pastor riding off into the sunset. These are real stories of real ministry, narratives of struggle and hope, limitation and failure. They are like photographs of birds in flight, opportunities to gaze for a brief moment at God intersecting in human lives that are in motion, stories of the interruptions and disruptions of grace that, sometimes in almost small and unnoticed ways, open people to a new future.

As Honeycutt describes his ministry, woven into these stories of contemporary saints and sinners, seekers and avoiders, the grief-stricken and heavy-laden are the stories of the Bible. In the way he tells these scriptural narratives—and this is a second sign of his pastoral imagination—there is no breach, no hermeneutical divide, between us and the people of the Bible. The biblical characters are the same fragile vessels for the holy as are the people who will nestle into the pews next Sunday. Moreover, Honeycutt never boils down the rich brew of the Bible so that it will pour neatly into the tiny thimbles of our world-weary, domesticated, and impoverished religious imaginations. Instead, in his hands the Bible makes us larger. He sets the Bible dancing, beckoning us to be swept up into the awe, energy, and wonder available to those who join the dance.

Like other ministers who possess pastoral imagination, Honeycutt doesn't allow his gaze to drift too far or too long into abstractions but instead finds profundity and a plentiful, if sometimes troubled, joy in the weekly tasks of ministry and the ordinary moments of people's everyday lives. For Honeycutt, as a Christian minister, the pastoral imagination is also an incarnational imagination, not a retreat from the material and tangible but a rediscovery in every experience that the Word repeatedly becomes flesh and dwells among us (see John 1:14). In Wendell Berry's novel *Jayber Crow,* the pastor-like protagonist complains about preachers who lack this incarnational vision:

> This religion that scorned the beauty and goodness of this world was a puzzle to me. To begin with, I didn't think anybody believed it. Those world-condemning sermons were preached to people who, on Sunday mornings, would be wearing their prettiest clothes. . . . The people who heard those sermons loved good crops, good gardens, good livestock and work animals and dogs; they loved flowers and the shade of trees, and laughter and music; some of them could make you a fair speech on the pleasures of a good drink of water or a patch of wild raspberries. While the wickedness of the flesh was preached from the pulpit, the young husbands and wives and the courting couples sat thigh to thigh, full of yearning and joy, and the old people thought of the beauty of the children. And when church was over they would go home to heavenly dinners of fried chicken, and creamed new potatoes and creamed new peas and hot biscuits and butter and cherry pie and

sweet milk and buttermilk. And the preacher, having foresworn on behalf of everybody the joys of the flesh, would eat with unconsecrated relish.[2]

This incarnational vision creates for Honeycutt a tension between the church as it is and the church that God is bringing into being. Places matter, time matters, memories matter, and yet Honeycutt won't allow these realities to forestall the ever-beckoning outward journey of faith. He tenderly confesses, "I used to love praying alone in the church sanctuary following worship after everyone had departed for Sunday lunch. It was good to rest for a few minutes in the quiet of the space, old oak pews occasionally creaking in the silence, recovering from the carried weight of Sunday assembly." And yet, he says that he is finally not content to remain there because the gospel keeps pressing him and his people outward and beyond, into the wider world of need, and into the possibilities for experiencing God that transcend any one sacred place.

It is no surprise that the spine that holds all of the material together in this book is the same constant reality that unified and symbolized Honeycutt's whole ministry: the weekly sermon. This volume isn't a textbook on preaching, but it could serve as one, because Honeycutt returns again and again to the craft of sermonizing. For Honeycutt, this comes not so much because he values this one act of ministry over all others, but because all other acts of ministry are refracted through the prism of preaching. Everything good and necessary about the ministry passes through the busy intersection of the sermon: the obedient hearing of Scripture, the love of and care for the people, the attending to the cries of the oppressed, and the challenge of the gospel to mount up with wings as eagles.

And—oh, yes—there's at least one other aspect of the pastoral imagination that we see in Honeycutt: the unmistakable solitariness of ministry. There is a curious, almost amusing verse in Mark's Gospel: "When [Jesus] was alone, those who were around him along with the twelve asked him about the parables." Alone, with people all around. That's ministry, and Honeycutt speaks of this when he says, "Pastors sign on for a career of feeling a little out of sync with the good people we are called to lead. Perhaps the idea of pastor as 'stranger' should be replaced with the idea of pastor as simply strange."

But it is this strangeness, this out-of-sync-ness, this solitude that allows for the angular perception that is always taken by those with pastoral imagination. They see things oddly, differently, illuminated by an uncommon light. It allows pastors like Honeycutt to lead God's people to places to which God is always calling, places these people can scarcely imagine, and, among pastors like Frank Honeycutt, one of our very best pastoral leaders, it empowers boldness.

In one of Giovannino Guareschi's witty novels about the meek little priest Don Camillo, he says of this timid pastor, "[W]henever he had to blow his nose in the middle of Mass he raised his eyes to Christ on the cross above the altar and silently prayed: 'Lord, help me blow my nose in a manner that will not cause a scandal!'"[3] In this book, however, we watch over Frank Honeycutt's shoulder as he goes about his ministry with tenderness, compassion, and long-suffering faith—but also and always with great courage.

Frank Honeycutt has pastoral imagination—and for this we can all be grateful.

> THOMAS G. LONG
> Bandy Professor Emeritus
> of Preaching
> Candler School of Theology
> Atlanta, GA

Introduction

I've always liked riding with Howard. Not because he drives the lead car and that's where someone like me is supposed to ride, but because he always has a story to share in the twenty-minute crawl at 15 mph between the church building and the old cemetery over on Elmwood Avenue. We are one of the few cities in the South that still allows funeral processions. I don't know how it works in other locales. Maybe everyone just jumps in their vehicles and gets to the graveyard as quickly as possible.

But here in South Carolina, we process. So, I tear off my sweaty robe after the last verse of "A Mighty Fortress," grab the Occasional Service book (the mini-version) my Aunt Flossie gave me after I graduated from seminary, and join Howard in the front seat. "Tell me something interesting in your line of work these days." He smiles, expecting the invitation, having heard me pose this opening a dozen times.

Howard's been at this for thirty years now. He's a solid man, speaks thoughtfully and slowly with the measured deliberation of poured pancake syrup. The funeral home positions him at the front door on visitation night like the welcoming

1

lion in front of the New York City Public Library—solid, comforting, consistent. He's seen it all. Clumps of mourners file by his sentry post to view the body and pay final respects. Howard knows just about everyone in town.

A couple years back, our mortuary, keeping up with the times, expanded their services to include pet funerals. I got a call from a church member once—Darlene. "Pastor, you gotta come now. Willy didn't make it. Sister was coming down them stairs about an hour ago in her favorite bathrobe, tripped about three steps from the bottom, and landed right on top of him. She's okay, nothing is broken, but you gotta come right now. She squashed the life right out of poor Willy, and there's no consoling her. She's wailing by the fire and asking for you. Can you come right now?"

My first cat funeral; Howard's third.

He ushers the weeping family into the black limousine directly behind our lead car with door closures so soft the clicks of noise could have been a quilt tucking the bereaved in for an afternoon nap. Howard pulls out into the main road next to our church building and slowly angles toward the first light and a waiting policeman, ready to stop all traffic for the procession.

A teenager in one of those godlessly-loud pickup trucks, mechanically adjusted for higher volume, roars through a yellow light. The officer shakes his head. I ask Howard why on God's green earth does a truck need to sound that loud? He laughs. "I told my wife recently that it's like pissing on your neighbor's geraniums." Or maybe saying "I'm alive, suckers" to unfortunates heading to a sad hole in the ground.

We're moving again. "You might be interested in a funeral we had last week," Howard says behind sunglasses. "Our first time releasing birds."

I hate releasing birds. I once presided over a wedding for a young couple whose family spent a ton of money on an elaborate outdoor wedding. They said their vows, we offered a blessing, and listened to a taped Dan Fogelberg song while staring at our feet. After a passionate kiss (which included a fairly long connective string of saliva that only I could see), avian foolishness followed. The birds were released three times and never got above the tree line, floating back to earth each time with leaden wings—an omen for a marriage that dissolved six months later. The last release included a futile upward push from one of the ushers.

Cars in the opposite lane slow down and even pull off the road, an old courtesy in the South. "Well, they got Linda's ashes in the ground okay at the Turner family plot," Howard tells me. "You know, that family goes way back in the county. The pastor read something poetic from Khalil Gibran and then Linda's husband released a dove from a shoe box equipped with a couple of air holes. My colleague, Sally (you'd like her), read about the symbolism of doves in the Bible—peace, security, the afterlife, all that. It was a beautiful day, and the dove made a long, slow loop around the cemetery. We all followed it, eyes skyward. Well, on the second loop a hawk suddenly shoots out from the trees, grabs the squawking bird in its claws, and flies into the woods at the far end of the lot for an early lunch. Audible gasp. Sally turns to me and whispers, 'Well, we're never doing *that* again.'"

We arrive at the cemetery. All goes well. A grandchild chokes out a poem she's written. The graveside liturgy includes Saint Paul's famous in-your-face declaration, "O death, where is thy sting?" I've often wondered how mourners truly feel about this startling question, surrounded by hundreds of gravestones that must have stung mightily for many. I make a mental note to ask Howard what he thinks about this question. Maybe we'll talk about it in the car on the way back to the church.

* * *

A pastor in North Carolina, a young woman of my acquaintance two years out of seminary, phoned me one recent Tuesday morning and left a message. "Can we talk sometime? I'm free this afternoon at three. Can you possibly call me then?"

I'd been Susan's[1] pastor at one time and had taken a role in her formation as a young Christian, participating in her eventual decision to enter seminary. She's one of the most solid and promising pastoral candidates I have ever assisted in the process leading to ordination—with all the gifts that might suggest a long and effective ministerial career.

We talked that afternoon at three and caught up, initially, on respective family details. The conversation then turned to challenges I'd heard described by many young pastors in the last few years: unrealistic expectations from church leadership; unresolved conflict centering on a previous pastor or staff person; inconsistent weekly offerings that quickly created serious budget deficits, including the inability to pay church employees; few friendships outside a grueling work week; a perceived lack of support from an overworked ecclesiastical oversight staff who live several hours away; and the worry of paying back large student loans.[2]

I asked about all the obvious: her prayer life; time reserved for regular exercise; the health of her marriage. Susan was doing all the right things and experiencing some of the fruits such disciplines bring a person over time. Her main worry: that no matter how much she did as a pastor for the people of her parish, nothing much was going to change.

We reached a point in the conversation that was filled with a good bit of silence. And then she asked, "Did you ever think about quitting?"

* * *

I arrived at seminary in 1981 for summer Greek, a month after our wedding, filled with excitement, but also with so many questions about my faith (and so many doubts) that I was certain the faculty would kick me out before the end of the first semester. "Perhaps my greatest breakthrough with regard to belief," writes Kathleen Norris, "came when I learned to be as consciously skeptical and questioning of my disbelief and doubts as I was of my burgeoning faith."[3] I love this quote, but in 1981—especially after watching a couple of classmates arrive confidently on campus with a full set of multicolored ordination stoles—I was far from embracing my catalog of doubt as healthy (or even helpful) for the pastoral life ahead.

In 1987, two years after graduating from seminary, I suffered a full-blown bout of clinical depression that was somewhat fueled (I later discovered) by a long genetic history on my mother's side of the family. Managed with the help of an excellent counselor, medication, and a supportive wife, my depression was definitely triggered by unrealistic pastoral expectations and inconsistent spiritual disciplines that created a pretty perfect storm. And yes, I told Susan, I had thought very seriously about quitting.

Quitting became a real option for me in the wake of (and recovery from) the almost year-long depression. The soul-crunching challenges that often face seminary graduates are somewhat different today, but many remain the same, especially the large mistake of neglecting to cultivate an inner spirit (shaped by the classic disciplines) that can stand up to "the authorities and powers of this present darkness" (Eph. 6:12) that infiltrate congregational life with no less frequency than any other earthly arena. Jesus's first encounter with evil in his public ministry was not in an obviously dark location, after all, but rather in a religious setting (Mark 1:21–28).

This is not to say that the spiritual development of a new pastor is without its own set of murky pitfalls. Advises the diabolical Uncle Screwtape to his nephew, Wormwood, a novice in the deceptive arts,

> Keep his mind on the inner life. He thinks his conversion is something *inside* him and his attention is therefore chiefly turned at present to the states of his own mind—or rather to that very expurgated version of them which is all you should allow him to see. . . . You must bring him to a condition in which he can practice self-examination for an hour without discovering any of those facts about himself which are perfectly clear to anyone who has ever lived in the same house with him or worked in the same office.[4]

With that warning caveat, I can say I have never met a pastor effectively immersed in this odd vocation for the long haul who is not attentive to centuries-old spiritual disciplines. At the end of the day, they have no saving value, but they do give the Spirit room to get at followers of Jesus and change us over time.

Sometime after my brush with depression (and with the assistance of helpful homiletic guides[5] along the way), it suddenly became clear to me that the process of writing and delivering a weekly sermon brought together a variety of spiritual disciplines in surprising synthesis. Perhaps this is an obvious no-brainer to most seminary graduates. For me, it was a light-bulb revelation that I either missed in school or that no one bothered to mention.

I cannot recall the author of this quote: "Ministry is not something you go and do. It is something you do as you go." Everything packed into that statement, a healthy description of Christian identity, can also find intersection with a pastor's developing identity as a preacher.

The development of an inner life, post-seminary, slowly began to lead to a resumption of joyful external encounters with parishioners like Howard, my friend who drives the lead funeral car. All conversations and moments—including un-cooperative doves, squashed feline unfortunates, annoyingly loud pickup trucks, and old questions from First Corinthians silently posed at a gravesite—are packed with preaching po-tential for a pastor who learns to pay attention and attempt to faithfully record the intrusions of the Spirit into a broken world, all of it indeed the Lord's (Ps. 24:1). These interrup-tions sometimes come to us loudly, and other times arrive whispered and obliquely, even accompanying the very doubt that once troubled me.

* * *

This book is written for pastors like Susan, recently out of seminary, who sometimes feel like giving up. My thesis is that the weekly act of preaching can be a remarkable gift that shapes the ongoing spiritual formation of both preachers and the congregations—often beset with what seem like insurmountable challenges—to which first-year pastors are often called.[6] (My first congregation included a misguided and vengeful woman whose palpable hold on my imagination caused me to turn around in transit to her house one night because I was convinced she meant to do me physical harm.)

The delivery of a weekly sermon requires intestinal fortitude. Regular preaching requires courage (a spiritual gift if you are born timid like me) as the pastor stands and says things offered in tandem with the Spirit's prodding. Jesus discovered this early in his ministry with folk who initially seemed to want him there (Luke 4:14–22), but after hearing a single sermon became miffed enough to try to interrupt his preaching ministry permanently (Luke 4:23–30). Before accepting a call, therefore, I have carefully checked the topography surrounding various churches I have served for nearby cliffs. (Kidding! Well, mostly.) It is a risky (and sometimes dangerous) conviction to actually believe "the spirit of the Lord is upon me" (Luke 4:18).

But the previous paragraph's lead sentence also applies to sermons that aren't necessarily prophetic and risky, but also inevitably comforting, or quizzical, or mutually agonizing in addressing shared suffering. A sermon's Sunday morning range is strategically limited by biblical theme and prescribed time, but the possibilities of finding intersection with human predicament and joy are overwhelmingly wide and varied over the length of a church year based upon ancient and endlessly revelatory stories. A preacher needs a process that regularly attempts to overhear where the Spirit is leading a congregation, bringing the listening to weekly articulation based upon a text first experienced long ago.

The pages that follow, starting with Monday's specific tasks, will be structured upon the ordered days of the week. I hope this process won't seem too regimented or legalistic, and I'm tempted to say "do whatever works for you" because I am largely an introvert—shying away from pointed advice that may smack of a seasoned preacher throwing a paternalistic arm around the shoulder of a newbie—and do not mean to suggest that one way works for all pastors, even though I am privately convinced of precisely that. (Again, kidding! Well, mostly.)

But I am indeed publicly convinced, over thirty years out of seminary, that most sermons do not effortlessly drop out of mid-air with little thought and no planning. Even if you resist naming the days up to delivery "a process," I hope you develop a few life-long homiletical habits from reading these pages.

And I also hope you continue to discover—even on the days you may feel like quitting—that congregations, including the most stubborn, need a preacher who wrestles (similar to Pastor Paul long before us, wondering at times about his own call) with a powerful set of timeless questions: "How are they to call on one in whom they have not believed? And how are they to believe in one of whom they have never heard? And how are they to hear without someone to proclaim him?" (Rom. 10:4).

1

MONDAY

Listening

Start Early

I think it was the great preacher Ernest T. Campbell[1] (1924–2010) who once observed that Sundays for a pastor come along as quickly as telephone poles outside the window of a moving train.

Even if Monday is your day off after an exhausting yesterday, spend half an hour with the coming Sunday's assigned lectionary texts. I realize that some traditions don't follow a lectionary, but will briefly say here that the lectionary is a tremendous gift to new pastors, forcing the novice preacher to reflect upon a large chunk of the Bible in the first three years out of seminary.[2] I invite you to strongly consider using the lectionary in your first years of preaching even if your tradition doesn't follow such a practice as a general rule.

A lectionary also offers the additional gift of avoiding the common accusation of "pushing your own biblical agenda" upon the congregation with a steady diet of your favorite texts. And we all have them. The lectionary will regularly expose you to fruitful preaching opportunities on texts you would probably never select on your own.

I'm thinking here of Jesus's odd teaching about repentance in Luke 13:1–9 (usually assigned in Lent, Cycle C), where he uses two strange local news stories—the slit throats of hapless Galileans and the unfortunate demise of those standing near the collapsing tower of Siloam—to warn his disciples about the dangers of delayed repentance. Jesus quickly covers the waterfront of most events regularly reported on the evening news: evil hatched by a despot, and tragedy involving innocents who happen to get in the way. It's a rather complicated and brief exchange between the master teacher and his students, even though its challenge is coupled with the gift of time requested by a persistent gardener in the accompanying parable.

This sort of pericope sends shivers, I suspect, down the spines of most new preachers. (At least that was true for me.) However, these are the very texts that parishioners wonder about while prowling around in the Bible's pages—much more than the rather straightforward truths of Psalm 23, for example. A lectionary often allows you to pull the elephant out of the closet and present the wily pachyderm in full view, even if you never apprehend (or comprehend) the large beast entirely.

At the very least, the lectionary affords an opportunity for preacher and congregation to engage together in an act of mutual consternation and head-scratching, immersed for the long haul in the Bible's full and wondrous corpus. I have always appreciated this description of our common journey from Rabbi Burton Visotsky:

> For the Rabbis and Church Fathers, reading the Book was an adventure, a journey to a grand palace with many great and awesome halls, banquet rooms, and chambers,

as well as many passages and locked doors. The adventure lay in learning the secrets of the palace, unlocking all the doors and perhaps catching a glimpse of the King in all his splendor.[3]

Over liturgical time, the lectionary will help you fall in love with even the Bible's unusual twists and strange turns that seek to intentionally shock our often-safe sensibilities.

Even though the lectionary offers a menu of four weekly texts, your Monday task (even if you have only thirty minutes) is to try to choose only one for your principal preaching text. A seasoned preacher may be able to balance more than one text in the scope of her sermon, but a single-text focus will teach a new preacher the knack of theme development.

Most sermons will benefit from the preacher's ability to write (cogently and privately) a single sentence describing the sermon's aim. If you find that on a regular basis you cannot do this with your sermons, it is likely that you're juggling too many themes.

A single preaching text increases the likelihood that you will remain focused in your sermon preparation and that your parishioners will remain focused as they listen. Jesus was very fond of the phrase "Let anyone with ears to hear listen." Sometimes preachers divert faithful listening by stuffing far too many items inside the ears of those who cannot possibly process them all. Barbara Brown Taylor learned about the wisdom of sermonic focus in a letter exchange with a friend:

> Last year I complained in writing to a friend that I was not sure people even listened to sermons anymore. She

wrote back, "I do think people are trying to listen and that preaching *does* matter. In fact, I think the vast majority of people are sitting in the pews with parched lips. They are so thirsty that they have lost their ability to listen, to speak, or to think. But one big gulp of Gatorade is not the answer. They will drown. Their thirst is so great that it requires a series of sips much like parched fields require a series of gentle rains."[4]

There will be other Sundays to use a provocative story or illustration that doesn't quite make the cut of your one-sentence theme statement. Try to see your ongoing preaching ministry as a "series of sips."

Choosing a single text may seem to contradict what I've just said about the merits of the lectionary's biblical breadth. The truth is that one text preached faithfully will increase the likelihood of a parishioner's private (or communal) investigation of the other supporting passages assigned for that Sunday.

Before moving on to other Monday tasks (or Tuesday, if you are taking Monday off), I offer a final word about the importance of early selection of a preaching text. It is my experience that the Holy Spirit rarely speaks instantly and when summoned. Good preaching relies on two words that find their origin in most kitchens: percolation and marination (heating and soaking). Fire and liquid are, incidentally, components of the Holy Spirit's functional sacramental DNA.

All pastors can share stories about a particularly trying week that unavoidably pushed sermon preparation until Saturday night. But this reality should be rare in practice because the Holy Spirit, by biblical definition, is rarely summoned on command. There is an unexpected and unruly nature to the Holy Spirit's specific manifestation in our lives.

Any prediction that Peter would find his tongue in the streets of a Jerusalem Pentecost fifty days after feeling tongue-tied (in the same streets!) would have been met with hoots of laughter and exchange of coin by anyone prone to first-century gambling. The Spirit is unpredictable and difficult to corral for urgent purposes. It therefore makes all the sense in God's world to start the sermon process early in the week with ears, eyes, and heart attuned to the Spirit's utterances all through the coming days in venues ranging from a moving car, to a hospital emergency room, to the back porch of an aging congregational matriarch, to your daughter's Thursday afternoon soccer game. The Spirit can certainly speak on Saturday night, but why waste the chances for holy intersections with the details of your week that might well begin on Monday?

Some practical advice: keep a writing pad and a pen close by, wherever you go, including both on a bedside table for "aha moments" that may awaken you during the night. The preaching process is often like gathering stray bits of bread along a path. You'll rarely find all the bread at once. And you won't use everything in a sermon that you write down in a given week. But once you've selected a text, your senses become attuned to the Spirit's nudges about it, which might occur . . . *anywhere*. You are the "recorder" for these irregular bits of inspiration. Be ready. What Anne Lamott observes about writing a novel can also be applied to writing a sermon:

E. L. Doctorow once said that "writing a novel is like driving a car at night. You can see only as far as your headlights, but you can make the whole trip that way." You do not have to see where you're going, you do not have to see your destination or everything you will pass along the way. You just have to see two or three feet ahead of you. This is right up there with the best advice about writing, or life, I have ever heard.[5]

Early text selection, an important Monday task, will not increase the Spirit's consistent penchant for holy communication. It will, however, increase a preacher's likelihood to faithfully record the communication.

The modern preacher's unfortunate temptation to reach for canned online sermons clearly preys upon a pastor's habits of delayed preparation, the Saturday-night panic button. "Only preachers who deliver their own sermons," writes Tom Long, "stand with one foot in the life of the people and one foot in the biblical text. No Internet preacher stands in this same place."[6] Parishioners will sense (over time) that you are indeed taking time to wrestle with God's word. Conversely, they'll also be able to detect when you are not.

If Monday isn't your day off, here are a few additional considerations in choosing a sermon text. (Otherwise, I invite you to conflate these considerations with your Tuesday tasks.)

Trust the Biblical Breadth of the Church Year

My phone call with Susan that afternoon revealed a number of challenging congregational issues. Any one of them was daunting; cumulatively, they seemed overwhelming (and would be for any pastor, regardless of age or experience).

Life in the mainline church has indeed changed since I graduated from seminary in 1985, over thirty years ago. Synodical seminary-tuition support for seminarians has largely dried up, leaving recent graduates with debt tension unheard of in previous generations of pastors. Local church offerings in general are down, creating anxiety for meeting staff payroll and worry, in some instances, about possible closure. Sunday worship attendance continues to shrink at alarming rates in most major Christian denominations. Congregational lay leaders often attach expectations to a new pastor that are unrealistic and wearing. The rise of the "Nones" (the Pew Research Center's term for the completely unaffiliated), especially in the twenty to forty range, often leaves young pastors with many congregants twice their age.[7]

The balance of this book will return to these issues often, especially as they impact the preaching ministry of recent seminary graduates. For now, consider how these issues may affect the Monday selection of a preaching text.

Topical sermons are rarely a good idea. As important as any of the issues named above happen to be, the topical sermon focused upon a "problem" or an "issue" usually deteriorates into a gripe session centering more upon the topic itself than God. The same danger is present in most "sermon series" meant to highlight a fetching or pressing subject near and dear to the human heart. (Deliver me from the sermon series devoted to "the love of grandparents.")

More advice: allow the biblical text to directly (or indirectly) raise the issue in question in a natural way. Again, the three-year lectionary offers the underrated gifts of time and pacing. Although our current church challenges are different from a generation ago, any "issue" you might name—lack of commitment, congregational depression, biblical infidelity, shifting allegiance, greed, injustice, abuse of power—will roll around in the lectionary over the course of three years. (And then we begin again.)

I have been asked, "Isn't there ever a time when a pastor might depart from the assigned lectionary text to address a pressing congregational issue?" My answer: "Perhaps." But I am also quick to say how many times (in a thirty-year ministry) I have gone foraging around both testaments for some applicable passage only to have the assigned texts offered within a specific church year season (more on that below) yield unexpected light on the very worries that sent me searching.

Sometimes the light surfaces obliquely. Sometimes the Spirit, somewhere between pulpit and listener, transforms my words in a healing direction I did not even intend.[8] Sometimes the text provides a cover and a shield from an incoming fusillade of responses. ("Hey, I didn't make this parable up," says the quick-footed pastor.) Trust the lectionary—in use in some form since the early centuries of the church and inherited from Judaism even earlier—even with your worry over "the big issues."

Regularly Check the Time

In one of her books,[9] Gertrude Mueller Nelson describes the fascinating origin of the Advent wreath in Scandinavia during the early Middle Ages. As the dwindling light of December prompted farmers to give thanks for the preceding harvest and bring tools and equipment inside a barn for cleaning and maintenance, families would also bring inside the house a single cartwheel and festoon the circle with lights and greenery, awaiting the Son who brings eternal light and life.

Nelson's book, as much about the power of measured and celebrated time as the history of a particular church season, offers an interesting insight about the wreath's practical (and visual) contribution to the season of slowing down: a family couldn't go anywhere on three wheels.

One Advent I led a children's sermon using a miniature car with rubber wheels. Removing one, wordlessly, I decorated the wheel with small sprigs of greenery and secured four birthday candles to the top of the wheel with a bit of Plasti-Tak, my go-to home adhesive—and, presto, a miniature Advent wreath. The sermon received a big laugh when I playfully encouraged the children to honor the spirit of the season by removing (with adult help) a Michelin from Mom's Mitsubishi, then hanging the tire from the rafters with lights and braided mistletoe. Maybe that would finally slow down mom, dad, and the whole family in memorable preparation for Christ's Advent.

A pastor's preaching text is always selected within a context that is wondrously cyclical and biblically imagined. There is really no need to scamper around the pages of the Bible in search of just the right text that might address some specific, pressing, nagging issue that occasionally awakens you in the night. We already have a story of salvation and truth—wonderfully arranged through centuries of calendar use—that addresses any situation that "the father of lies" (John 8:44) might deceptively cast our way.

The church year systematically arranges the story for handy homiletical planning. In the time you've allotted for Monday text selection, also take a few moments to ask the old question posed by God to the Garden's first inhabitants: "Where are you?" (Gen. 3:9). This is obviously much more than a geographical question. God knew their location. The question centers upon personal (and corporate) awareness. *Where are you? What time is it? What's occurring in your life that seems more important than God?*

The church year thrusts the ontological clock in our faces with rapt repetition. "You have died," claims Colossians 3:3. "You've been baptized into his death," suggests a rather stark declaration in Romans 6:3. "I have been crucified with Christ; and it is no longer I who live, but Christ who lives within me" (Gal. 2:19–20). Perhaps we know these claims on some sacramental level. But the repetition of a Lenten ashen cross (circling back to the genesis of that divine Genesis question), traced repeatedly over many years on a recurring Wednesday in remembrance of baptism, rubs a congregation's collective nose in death and ash with such utter regularity that our great fear of no longer breathing some day slowly diminishes and ceases to have the dark hold on God's people that it once did.

This may sound utterly obvious, but it has given me courage to preach on many occasions: our attempts at words are offered from within an ongoing story, told repeatedly in cycles over the centuries, of which we are only a part. Far from diminishing a pastor's personal sermonic efforts, the realization empowers and strengthens him or her.

German novelist Michael Ende (1929–1995) tells the story of young Bastian, an ostracized boy who often hides in the school attic to read and retreat from the taunts of classmate bullies. Bastian discovers a strange book that makes him sense that he's more than just a reader—he's an actual character in the narrative. Every time he pulls back from the tale, the action of the plot is interrupted. The book continues its pace only when Bastian fully engages the plot as an actual character in the story.[10]

Bastian's experience reminds me a bit of the elliptical ending to the Gospel of Mark, which concludes with the women fleeing from the tomb. "They said nothing to anyone, for they were afraid" (Mark 16:8). The story promises its resumption only when the disciples make a commitment to rejoin the original mission of Jesus in Galilee (Mark 16:7). In short, the story is starting over again.[11] This is our choice also: flee or engage.

Monday-morning text selection is greatly assisted by considering two questions: "What time is it?" And "Where are you?" These may be the two primary questions engendered by the gift of the church year as a preacher begins the week.

2
TUESDAY

Hearing

Pray the Sighs

Pastors sigh for a variety of reasons. Cumulative sadness often surfaces the sigh after we've endured weeks of bad news. Periods of time when we have far too much to do (and not enough hours to effectively address the challenges) elicit frequent sighs. When pastors realize that opportunity (what could have been) has come and gone in the lives of those we love, we usually sigh a lot. In cars at traffic lights, at desks in offices on Monday mornings, or late at night, poised over sink suds with laundry awaiting attention—clergy are often overworked people whose sighs reveal quite a bit.

"You must have had a hard day," says my good wife.

"What makes you say that?" I want to know.

"Well, you sighed."

"I did not."

"Well, I just heard you," she says.

Sighs often reveal one's emotional state faster and better than words. Something unspoken is brooding in us. If there were some sort of "sigh-ometer" that could count the number of times we exhale daily in this fashion, pastors of any age might be surprised.

Just after a short break in the seacoast town of Tyre, where he reluctantly listens to (and ultimately grants) the request of a panicked mother, Jesus scoots up the shoreline about twenty miles to Sidon and then into the region of the Decapolis, where he offers an audible sigh (Mark 7:34) to God as he heals a deaf man with a speech impediment. The story reports that this exhalation of breath occurs in conjunction with "looking up to heaven," so I'm interpreting the sigh as an earthy prayer.

I'm intrigued by this. Before he offers words to God, Jesus offers God his guts. He doesn't sugar-coat his petitions with a lot of polite "Almighty Everlastings," pretending to be on his best behavior (like I often am) during prayer. Jesus strips away all semblance of devotional etiquette and *sighs* to God.

In the book of Romans, Saint Paul says, "The Spirit helps us in our weakness; for we do not know how to pray as we ought, but that very Spirit intercedes for us with sighs too deep for words" (8:26). Pretty remarkable evidence: the second and third persons of the Holy Trinity are found sighing in the Bible.

What would happen if we tried to become conscious of our sighs and where they come from, especially as they find intersection with a sermon beginning to form in our imagination? What if we perceived a sigh as the most fundamental and basic of prayers? Try praying wordlessly sometime soon with only sighs and see what happens; note what images come to mind.

After all, it is the breath (wind) of God that swept over the waters in Genesis with creative force. It was the breath of God that formed the first humans in Eden. It was the breath of God that knocked over tables and set the church on fire at Pentecost. Perhaps the breath we offer *back* to God in the form of prayerful, audible sighs also has the creative force to bring brooding words to the surface for a sermon. Maybe it's the faithful sigh toward heaven that signals to God our willingness to be partners in change. Jesus looks up to heaven and sighs—prayer without adornment. By giving his breath back to God, he stands open to breathe *in* the will of God.

And please note that at this point in his life, on and near the coast of Tyre and Sidon,[1] Jesus still seems to be discerning the implications of the divine will—which might explain his rather erratic behavior with a Syrophoenician woman in the preceding story (Mark 7:24–30). He basically says, "Look, lady, I feel for your situation and everything, but you're not one of us, not our kind. I've got a specific job description here that spells out exactly the people I'm supposed to help, and I'm really sorry and everything, but you're just not on that list. Now could you please leave?" It's a rather terse interaction no matter how one tries to explain it.

Jesus eventually heals this woman's daughter, but it must be said that she and her kind were not on Jesus's radar screen at first. She (like the deaf man) was a foreigner. Jesus originally felt called only to the children of Israel. But God was in the process of scrambling that perception in Jesus. Perhaps the man sighed multiple times as he changed directions.

The healing of the deaf man follows directly on the heels of the reluctant ocean-front encounter. Jesus looks up to heaven, sighs, and implores, "*Be opened.*" Certainly, he means the man's ears. But isn't it possible that Jesus is also praying that he might be "open" to this new ministry toward foreigners and outsiders?

Note that Jesus uses saliva liberally, medicinally, with the speech healing. He was brought within "spitting distance" of people he once considered outsiders. Perhaps he was beginning to understand where this new mission, this boundary-crossing, might lead. In the very next chapter of Mark, Jesus predicts his death in detail for the first time (8:31). Radical ministry to outsiders can get you killed. That indeed called for a sigh.

Perhaps a mark of our own faithfulness as pastors is that we sigh a lot. Something is dying, and something new is being brought to life. Listen for these kingdom sighs. What is dying in your congregation in order to make room for new life? What areas of life together is the Holy Spirit brooding over, sighing over?

Something wasn't settled in Jesus. He sighed. Pay attention to your own sighs—where they come from; what they might be telling you; how they might signal change and intersect with the sighs of parishioners in your congregation.

Then pray your sighs, especially as you begin the process leading to Sunday's sermon. Don't worry about the words of the sermon just yet. Allow the text that you've chosen for Sunday to begin its work of percolation and marination through your prayer life.

Get Outside

Before moving on to crafting a sermon based upon your specific preaching text for the coming Sunday, consider also the prayer context into which you bring the various sighs that seem to be bubbling forth from the pastoral depths. Some advice: get outside the church building for regular prayer, and take your preaching text along with you.

I used to love praying alone in the church sanctuary following worship after everyone had departed for Sunday lunch. It was good to rest for a few minutes in the quiet of the space, old oak pews occasionally creaking in the silence, recovering from the carried weight of Sunday assembly.

Preaching and leading worship (followed by a long receiving line that usually includes various mentions of news and need) is often exhausting, and hard to fully describe for friends who've never done it. I enjoyed sitting in a pew afterwards, looking toward the pulpit and altar, giving thanks for other pastors who'd preceded me, taking a few notes for pastoral follow-up, and reflecting upon the events of the morning. It was good to be surrounded by the names of those etched into the surrounding stained glass, now part of the communion of saints in light.

Church worship spaces are, of course, wonderful places to pray. But prayer limited only to such space can unconsciously contain the direction of a sermon in rather locally specific ways, subtly segregating a certain congregation's needs and challenges from what God is doing in the wider world.

I have always found it interesting that Jesus's first encounter with the demonic in his public ministry was in a worship setting (see Mark 1:21–28), a local parish, not in some obviously evil locale that made the evening news. New pastors shouldn't make too much of this, but neither should the surprising context be dismissed. The chatty voices intending to derail Jesus's teaching ministry in Mark's Gospel emerge only after a specific connection is made to a higher authority beyond that of established religious protocol and local custom (the scribes). Jesus teaches with authority, and "just then" (1:23) a disruptive man with an attitude and agenda emerges.

Perhaps it's unwise to connect this man even playfully with your most annoying troublemaker in congregational life. (But I would forgive you if you did; I've met my share of rather toxic church members whose erratic spiritual behavior gave me pause.) Maybe it's enough to say that worship spaces aren't automatically tension-free just because they're often called "sanctuaries."

Pastors are certainly called to serve creatively and faithfully in specific locations with a street address, but varying the context for prayer leading up to the sermon may be a more important part of the preaching process than one might think. I especially want to lobby for getting outside. My four pastoral calls in thirty-one years of ministry were unique and different, but each offered this in common: a setting that afforded nearby escape from the regular hum and rhythm of a church building.

After seminary, my first call in the Shenandoah Valley was near the national park and its many opportunities for quick isolation. The next fourteen years found our family at the other end of Virginia in a community (Abingdon) that had just converted an old railroad line into a biking and hiking path that eventually meandered through the nearby town of Damascus and intersected there with the Appalachian Trail. I can't tell you how many times I got out of the church building and walked the "path to Damascus." The next stop (almost ten years) in the inner city of Columbia, South Carolina, afforded a five-minute drive to a canal-walk where I could observe an astonishing amount of wildlife and water (even at flood stage) belting down an ancient channel at the confluence of two rivers. My final parish setting in the small, upstate South Carolina town of Walhalla, where I now live in retirement, is close to a still-underused resource called the Foothills Trail, seventy-five miles in length, and a national scenic waterway, the Chattooga River.

Getting out of the church building with your preaching text for the coming Sunday clears away (at least temporarily!) the cobwebs from a multitude of meetings and offers fresh perspective through the creative realities of the first article of the Apostles' Creed.

If a sermon is an act of creation authored by the Holy Spirit, it makes all the sense in the world to take a few notes about a sermon while out in creation itself. The preacher recalls in nature the awesome divine imagination of the One who hatched the astonishing diversity of the cosmos. Taking sermon notes in a natural setting will lead a pastor, over time, to describe a God who is involved in a far larger project than the concerns of a particular congregation alone, though those concerns are certainly included. Parishioners will encounter in Scripture a much longer view of life beyond that of "my family, my country, my church." Praying outside never fails to widen my preaching panorama.

What fiction writer Benjamin Percy says of his stories can also be applied to a preacher and Sunday sermons that attempt to enter old Bible narratives: "When a reader first picks up a story, they are like a coma patient—fluttering open their eyes in an unfamiliar world, wondering, *where am I, when am I, who am I?* The writer has an obligation to quickly and efficiently place the reader in the story."[2]

Percy's thoughts about narratives occurring in a specific context are especially accurate in an era when sermons might assist parishioners who are increasingly unfamiliar with the Bible's wide scope. Getting outside for part of the process leading to a sermon can be a great help in opening the preacher's imagination to finding language that might help loosen a local parish from a climate that has become spiritually stultifying. Take a walk with your preaching text.

Before moving on to other Tuesday tasks, I want to offer two additional thoughts on getting outside for prayer:

Leave the Cell Phone in the Car

You can do without the thing for at least an hour per day, no matter how "on call" you wish to be for members of the church. Stanley Hauerwas once whimsically described a typical pastor as "a quivering mass of availability." It is important to be available to others, but certainly not at the expense of a pastor's availability to God.

Essayist Andrew Sullivan, in a powerful confessional essay describing his own "distraction sickness" in work that almost killed him, writes,

> Just look around you—at the people crouched over their phones as they walk the streets, or drive their cars, or walk their dogs, or play with their children. . . . Visit an airport and see the sea of craned necks and dead eyes. We have gone from looking up and around to constantly looking down. . . . If churches came to understand that the greatest threat to faith today is not hedonism but distraction, perhaps they might begin to appeal anew to a frazzled digital generation.[3]

Take Along a Few Note Cards

Record images and ideas that might emerge as you encounter your preaching text outside in prayer. Preachers need to be ready to record divine transmission when the Spirit speaks to us. You won't use all of these prayer jottings in the Sunday sermon, but it will normally be in your prayer time that a sermonic theme will begin to emerge. Given a pastor's regular and sometimes zany changes of direction in a given day, memory alone is notoriously unreliable. Again, I quote writer Anne Lamott, who maintains that insights will usually escape irretrievably down a variety of rabbit holes if we aren't ready to record them:

> I think that if you have the kind of mind that retains important and creative thoughts—that is, if your mind still works—you're very lucky and you should not be surprised if the rest of us do not want to be around you. I actually have one writer friend—whom I think I will probably be getting rid of soon—who said to me recently that if you do not remember it when you get home, it probably wasn't that important.[4]

Sermons will not appear all at once unless you've copped-out and subscribed to a weekly on-line sermon service (which, as I have earlier suggested, is not really biblical preaching at all). Withdraw alone without a phone; pray over your chosen text; and be ready to record insights. There is more to preaching an effective sermon than these three imperatives. But faithful sermons certainly begin here.

Play with the Text

The balance of this chapter (tasks for Tuesday, but certainly possible other days of the week) will focus upon engaging your preaching text during the regular duties of a pastoral day—on the go, in other words: in hospital rooms and nursing homes, on back porches, and at stoplights.

The first portable homiletical habit is what I like to call "playing with the text." Jewish Bible scholars who engage in the ancient interpretive art of "midrash" take great delight in examining these ancient stories from lots of odd (but faithful) angles—positing amusing questions, considering hypothetical outcomes, and wondering why a certain word was chosen over another. The old stories of the Bible have staying power not because the word "Holy" is usually affixed to the spine of a book in which the stories are housed. The Bible comes alive in any century as we locate our lives in the narrative.

Someone once likened the century-jumping electricity inherent in the Bible's "living word" to looking out a living room window at a certain scriptural scene acted out in the viewer's backyard. At some point, the person viewing the scene recognizes her reflection in the window through which she was earlier just gazing at the action; her own face is now transposed into the scene. This, ideally, is the aim of any sermon based upon a text that is centuries old. We keep telling the stories because their truths impact our lives in profound ways as old insights intersect with a new audience, in some ways creating a new story.

I have always loved how North Carolina Baptist preacher Carlyle Marney (1916–1978), after a public lecture in a university setting, once responded to a student's question concerning the existence of the Garden of Eden. "Believe in it? I have actually been there. It is at 215 Elm Street in Knoxville, Tennessee." The student heatedly insisted that the Garden, according to the details in the Bible, was probably located somewhere in Asia. Marney replied with a classic example of his own gaze reflected upon the story's old window:

> Well, you couldn't prove it by me. For there [in Knoxville], on Elm Street when I was but a boy, I stole a quarter out of my mama's purse and went down to the store and bought me some candy and I ate it. And then I was so ashamed that I came back and hid in the closet. It was there that she found me and asked, "Carlyle, where are you? Why are you hiding? What have you done?"[5]

Bible commentaries will be important allies in the process leading up to writing a sermon, but use caution in relying upon them too early in the week. It's probably wise to go to commentaries with your questions about a text rather than seeking answers for the sermon's direction. Creatively "playing" with the details of a Bible text can bring new life to a sermon process that may have become rather stale and rote.

Before rushing to discover an expert's interpretation, take time to note how you feel about the text you've chosen. What may be weird about this slice of Scripture that a parishioner may also find odd in Sunday public proclamation? What strikes you as amusing or out-of-step in the telling of the story? How do you think the characters sounded? Why? (More to come on this last question. For now, note that you can easily test possible textual intonation on the go, in a moving car, on the way to your next visit.)

Consider the old story of "the woman at the well" in John 4:1–41. The story is normally offered in Cycle A from the lectionary during the season of Lent. These old, lengthy stories in John—additionally those of Nicodemus, "the man born blind," and the raising of Lazarus in chapters 3, 9, and 11, respectively—were once used to instruct adults seeking baptism in a three-year catechetical process. Candidates were invited to examine the rich narratives from multiple theological angles in the forty days of Lent preceding their watery welcome at the Great Easter Vigil. It was early textual "play," in other words.

After her honest (and surely embarrassing) encounter with Jesus, the woman departs the well, approaches her neighbors, and says, "Come and see a man who told me everything I have ever done!" (John 4:29). This woman seems absolutely beside herself about a man who told her the truth about her life, including the sordid parts. As a preacher looks through the backyard window at this story acted out, it might be fruitful to ask: Would you be excited about someone who could see right through you like that? Who could cut through all the excuses and alibis to see who you really are—the good, the bad, and the ugly?

Recall an important detail. It is high noon (4:6). File away the time of day. Jesus sits by an old well. He's worn out from his journey, parched and thirsty. The sun beats down unmercifully on the Samaritan city of Sychar.

What is Jesus doing here anyway? Samaria isn't his home. In fact, Samaritans were the sworn enemies of his people. He's woefully out of place sitting there, sticking out like a sore thumb. Even though Jesus once told a parable of a "good" Samaritan, that was just the point. In the eyes of first-century

Jewish folk, there *were not* any good Samaritans. Jesus is sitting beside a well where he has no business sitting. The text says he "had" (4:4) to go through Samaria on his way back to Galilee, but it's actually not the quickest way home from the events described in chapter three. The verb implies theological urgency, not geographical ease via MapQuest.

This is the longest conversation Jesus will have with anybody in any of the Gospels. Longer than any single recorded chat he had with his mother, for example. "Those who drink of the water that I will give them will never be thirsty," says Jesus. "The water that I will give will become in them a spring of water gushing up to eternal life" (4:14).

"I will take some of that," says the woman.

The story could've easily ended right there, if you ask me. Jesus crosses two sets of tracks. She is a woman *and* a Samaritan, doubly an outsider. Those facts alone make a powerful point. Jesus has something; the woman asks for it. Why can't that be enough? I say end the story right there. But watch how Jesus begins to tap into the woman's real thirst. Recall again the hour.

"Go, call your husband," he says. That little request hangs in the air for what seems like eternity. For Jesus somehow knows *everything* about this woman. He can see right through her.

The weird thing, noted by the preacher praying over this old text, is that this woman seems *utterly unburdened* by this strange cross-examination at the public well. "Come and see a man who told me everything I have ever done!" This is what she tells her neighbors, who, knowing her past, really must have raised their eyebrows at such an invitation.

While toying around with this text, I write this note in the margin: one of the reasons that healing may be delayed in any of us is that we never come to terms with our "secrets" from the past. We think we can bury them, hide them—even from God.

"He told me everything I have ever done." I suppose this could be an incredibly frightening statement. But for this long-ostracized woman, it seems like an amazingly liberating declaration. She is absolutely ecstatic that someone has bothered to know her so fully and still love and accept her, warts and all. After meeting Jesus, she evangelizes the whole town.

It was also high noon on a hill many Fridays ago when they nailed Jesus to a tree: the Lamb of God, who takes away the sin of the world. The man who tells me the truth about myself when others will not. The man who offers love and new direction in spite of anyone's past.

Ponder Truth Told "Slant"

As the new preacher gets used to playing with old Bible texts (as you just did in John 4), encountering them in a way that is somewhat liberating from the more serious (and absolutely necessary) encounter with the Bible in the technical commentaries, it is also instructive to notice how Jesus regularly goes about springing the truth on his listeners—his rather cagey strategy of truth-telling.

In one of her poems, Emily Dickinson says, "Tell all the truth, but tell it slant." What did she mean by this? Rare is the person who boldly says, "I want you to tell me directly the ugly truth about myself." My loving wife will tell you that I generally run the opposite way from a difficult truth about my personality. I suspect most of us have this in common.

My oldest daughter is a public defender in Columbia, South Carolina. Her life's work often involves trying to out the truth with people who have a vested interest in hiding it.

Jesus knew this about his listeners, of course. He knows it about us. He was steeped in old stories like the one about a privileged king who saw a beautiful woman bathing and wanted her so badly that he arranged for the woman's husband to be killed in battle (2 Sam. 11:1–12:15). Nathan's strategy in confronting David for such despicable behavior is a great example of "truth told slant." He can't come directly at the king with a wagging finger. He might figuratively lose that finger at the hands of such a powerful and high-spirited man. Instead, Nathan tells a story—truth told artfully and with a strategy—that slowly reveals David's sin in a way that a thousand "thou shalt nots" would never begin to touch. Nathan's strategy works and leads the king to pen arguably the most powerful confessional psalm (Psalm 51) in the corpus. The psalm actually includes an introductory note linking the verses to the event.

Just after the violence involving white supremacists in Charlottesville (in August 2017), Tina Fey appeared on *Saturday Night Live* and proceeded to devour an entire sheet cake while commenting upon the tragedy. Fey, a graduate of the University of Virginia and perhaps more closely associated with the ugly events of past days than most, succeeded in gaining a larger audience that was truly listening to the truths she was sharing (between maniacal bites of cake) because she avoided coming at her listeners directly with a barrage of moral invective. I thought *The Daily Beast* completely missed Fey's brilliant satire when the opinion website tweeted, "Tina Fey's 'Eat Cake' Strategy After Charlottesville Is Bad Advice." Really?

Several summers ago, I was in Chicago walking downtown on Michigan Avenue and encountered a street preacher who was railing at passersby with a variety of loud topics. No one paid him any attention. I had some time and decided to stop and listen for a while—I actually looked right at him and listened for about twenty minutes. I was surprised that what he was saying found at least a bit of intersection with my own theological convictions. But no one heard him that day. Any truth he might have been sharing was lost in the shrill volume of his words. I am reminded here of a culinary connection:

> In Japan, chefs offer the flesh of the puffer fish, or *fugu*, which is highly poisonous unless prepared with exquisite care. The most distinguished chefs leave just enough of the poison in the flesh to make the diner's lips tingle, so that they know how close they are coming to their mortality. Sometimes, of course, a diner comes *too* close, and each year a certain number of *fugu*-lovers die in midmeal.[6]

When God spoke in the night to the boy Samuel long ago, he said, "I am about to do something in Israel that will make both ears of anyone who hears of it tingle" (1 Sam. 3:11). Great change was afoot in the house of Eli, but there was no need for shouting. Effective preaching dances along an important border between pastoral and prophetic. "Let your speech always be gracious, seasoned with salt" (Col. 4:6). Some salty speech is good; too much is overpowering. Like good cooking, preaching requires a delicate seasoning balance.

I'm sure that Jesus just lost it sometimes and turned up the volume with his disciples and others. (The notable railing against the scribes and Pharisees in Matthew 23 comes to mind.) But his normal method of truth-telling is subtler, with even a delayed detonation in the lives of his listeners. Rarely does Jesus "explain" the meaning of his parables told delightfully slant. They are usually left tantalizingly open-ended. We never learn if the brothers reconcile after the prodigal returns home to an undeserved feast while the elder sibling stands outside with his arms crossed. We never discover if those who worked all day in the vineyard ever get over the scandal of equal pay for vastly unequal hours worked.

Jesus's teaching and preaching of difficult truths often have an elliptical feel, a dot-dot-dot tenor, because insight is rarely embraced all at once and right away by any of us. It creeps up on us gradually, in waves, over time. Lasting truth is told "slant" by wise communicators because listeners are usually just not ready to make the changes such truth demands all at once via the in-your-face style of that Chicago street preacher.

The form a preacher chooses to convey the truth of Christ need not involve something as flamboyant as Fey's sheet cake or even Nathan's clever story about the heist of a favorite ewe lamb. But the packaging of truth is important because we (all of us) have become pretty masterful at avoiding direct truth that often sounds shrill and legalistic. The art of truth-telling isn't something a beginning preacher learns all at once. But be thinking about this wise advice from a clever poet whose own communication style was undeniably angular: "Tell all the truth, but tell it slant."

Explore Tenor and Tone

A final Tuesday task involves making some decisions about how a text may have originally *sounded* to people who first heard it. This is especially important with texts that involve dialogue. Discerning vocal tenor in a story is a vital (but often overlooked) interpretive clue in developing a sermon theme. My advice: read the story aloud dozens of times throughout the week. Shut the door of your office. Take advantage of lulls at traffic lights. Ask the person with whom you've just shared home communion how they think a character in the story may have sounded.

Of course, we cannot know for sure how the words of Jesus (or any other Bible character) may have exactly sounded in tone and tenor, but it's important to try. Read the following words on this page, addressed to my son at age thirteen by his father: "Okay, Lukas, it's time to take out the garbage." A reader cannot know from the words alone whether I'm addressing my son with a gentle reminder, a firm reprimand, or even a sense of urgency because the garbage truck is a block away.

Consider this quote from God in the book of Amos. "I gave you cleanness of teeth in all your cities" (4:6a). Initially, it seems the Lord has watched benevolently over municipal dental health. Upon closer examination, when one speaks this line aloud in context, one realizes that God has actually judged the cities by withholding food so there's no need to brush teeth. The interpretive tenor here reveals a rather sassy God.

Tone and tenor are vital components of biblical interpretation. It took me a long time to discover the importance of such discernment in the process of preparing a sermon. Think of Jesus on the road to Emmaus with Cleopas and the other unnamed guy (Luke 24:13–35). The two men, heading away from the early Christian community, walk along the road disconsolately with a presumed stranger. We know the stranger is playing dumb about recent events with these two guys who finally, in exasperation, ask (in FGH translation), "Are you the only dunderhead in the whole city who doesn't know these things?"

Jesus responds with a two-word query (24:19): "What things?" How did Jesus pose this little question? What did it sound like? Was he indeed just playing with them? Testing their true motives in abandoning his fledgling movement? What were his own motives in remaining furtive? Was he just having a bit of fun at their expense?

In another post-Easter scene, Jesus is on the beach, starting a breakfast fire for fishermen who've returned to their old nets (John 21:1–14). They're not supposed to be out there on the sea, please recall. Jesus has given them clear marching orders to fish for people. Earlier, when it's dark outside, Peter says, "I am going fishing" (21:3). Did he say this with some naughty excitement? Or with sad resignation? Or maybe with a bit of boredom? Or for some other reason?

See also Jesus on the beach as the erstwhile fishermen first encounter their old friend, who at this point remains unknown to them. Jesus says, "Children, you have no fish, have you?" How do you think this first sounded? Is Jesus rather sassy here? Maybe withholding the divine "gotcha" for just a bit?

It's not so important that you get tone and tenor exactly right in a story. Preachers interpreting these ancient stories often cannot know for sure. But there is something about entering a story in this way that unlocks for the preacher a host of ideas from another part of the brain. Again, make sure you have pen and paper nearby as you recite a story aloud. Experimenting with tone and tenor will surface lots of leads for biblical preaching.

*   *   *

Much of what I've said in this chapter can be (and should be) accomplished outside the church office. Try to take your preaching texts into as many different venues as possible—contexts that are a regular part of your workweek. Use your preaching text for the coming Sunday in church-member homes, at hospital bedsides, in youth-group devotional periods. Let the text incubate in the hearts and minds of people you encounter all through the week. They'll enjoy knowing how they're assisting with your sermon preparation. Older people, small children, and others will be honored that you've bothered to ask them how a specific Bible character may have sounded in a certain situation. Homebound and hospitalized members who aren't able to worship with the wider community will feel included even though absent.

Take your text on the road. Church members, over time, will sense and see and hear the delight you take in preaching and find joy in the collaborative nature of proclaiming God's word.

On to Wednesday.

3

WEDNESDAY

Exegeting

Exegete Souls and Stories

When the weathervane atop the Lutheran church steeple points toward our local post office, snow is on the way. Our little town sits just south of the Blue Ridge escarpment in the northwest corner of South Carolina, not far from fairly tall mountains in a state known for beaches. It snows here most winters, six inches per season if we're lucky. School is cancelled. Milk and bread disappear from stocked shelves at Ingle's. Babies are made in the lull from work. It's an exciting time for southerners. People seem friendlier, oddly thawing when something frozen is on the way.

Between hospital visits when snow seemed certain, I used to lie down on the grass ("He makes me lie down in green pastures") in the side yard next to the church building, arms outstretched, pointing an extended index finger toward the mailroom on Church Street, viewable a few blocks north. Anna, our church secretary, would snap the picture, laughing as cars slowed down and honked at what the odd Lutheran pastor was doing now. She would tell me that the picture was a big hit on Facebook. Over two hundred *likes*. People like to see their pastor doing silly things. The Human Weathervane.

I wore a black wig once, briefly, during the homily at Charlie Sandifer's[1] memorial service, completely bucking the formality of a Lutheran funeral liturgy, because his daughter Debbie begged me to do it. People talked for weeks about the pastor wearing a wig for such a normally somber occasion, popping up in the pulpit at a strategic moment. I can't recall Jesus's specific teaching appointed for the service, or whether the words of our Lord had any connection at all to the bushy wig. Charlie used to answer the front door at his farm, wearing the long locks, to shock neighbors and delivery men. Debbie pleaded, almost tearfully, for its inclusion. It was her daddy's signature move. How could I turn her down?

"All is vanity!" warns the wise *Qoheleth* ("Teacher") repeatedly in Ecclesiastes. I read somewhere that "vanity" in Hebrew basically means flatulence—the gaseous pastor, full of hot air. I'm ready to lie down in another pasture where I'm not a pastor and no one knows me. I wore my clerical collar once at O'Hare in Chicago and vowed never to do that again. Even strangers love telling ministers their stories.

Nothing shocks me anymore. I nod much like a dog would and try to maintain consistent eye contact. A pastor friend in Virginia told me that he fell asleep one afternoon in his church office while listening to a woman pour out the details of her sad marriage. "You must not find this very interesting!" she told him.

I was fishing once on vacation at the beach, behind sunglasses, free as a bird and loving the anonymity of the coast. And then I saw them, Jay and David, members of our youth group back home, laughing and fishing for Atlantic spot eight benches down the pier. "Hey, it's Pastor Frank!" They showed me their catch. I love those two, but my cover was blown.

In a recurring dream, I climb our high pulpit only to discover that I've lost my sermon manuscript and can't find it anywhere, even after a thorough search at home and church and roadside ditches in-between. Clergy friends tell me their anxiety dreams involve appearing before the congregation without clothes—shamed, weary of hiding some embarrassing and probably rather innocent infidelity. Saint Peter went fishing in the nude late in the Gospel of John (21:7). He clearly wasn't supposed to be out in the waves after the Lord told him to give up nets and fish for people instead. *Caught.* Busted. In my dreams, I'm caught not with my pants down but with my words lost. Nothing left to say—mum, occasionally wearing the wig.

Sometimes, when the building was empty, I would climb up into the tall church steeple alone, high above the organ loft, avoiding the loud bell that gongs every hour on the hour, heard all over town. (I made that mistake once and had to cower in a corner with my ears covered.) Original hand-hewn chestnut timbers (1860, pre-blight) are still in view; impressive efforts of German ingenuity to get heavy logs up so high with only ropes and pulleys. From such a height I could see some of the craftsmen, the graves of the church's charter members.

My artist friend, Kent, carved a three-inch Quasimodo figure in his home studio, and we hid the hunchback in an old angled eave of the tower, just the little man's nose and eyes peeping out. It's quiet up there. In the distance beyond the post office, the row of mountain peaks, straddling the state line, looks much closer than the actual distance I have driven so many times. Once when I was hunched up there, avoiding a wasp's nest, I noticed the weathervane was only a few inches from my head on the other side of the roof shingles. I was almost wearing it, like a funny hat.

I once had to confront this man named Bruce, who was always leaving helpful notes in my church office mailbox like this one: "The homebound members in our parish just cannot understand why they're being neglected by you on such a regular basis." The notes were always a day-brightener.

Bruce used to work in surveillance in the DC area and fancies himself a Renaissance man, skilled in just about anything you could name. On Sundays after worship, he gives church visitors his business card, which lists various credentials: *Writer, Art Collector, Historian, Pilot.* I think he had seven titles on the last edition of the card. I daydream about adding *Pain in the Ass.* "Let me know if I can ever do anything for you," Bruce smiles with cocky confidence while distributing his colorful card. Nobody ever does. It's sad in a way, the wide and nervous bypass around his self-perceived brilliance.

Bruce once distributed to our Tuesday Morning Bible Study Group a short, self-published booklet he had penned primarily for his grandchildren, sagely titled *Advice for Young People.* He wanted our honest reaction. As the class was breaking up, I randomly flipped to page seven, where he had asserted, "Not that many young men know how to pleasure a woman." An asterisk after this statement led to a footnote offering various how-to books on this topic that he would gladly lend from his personal library to any interested inquirer. I pondered privately what Nettie Mae, who, at ninety-one, was the oldest member of our group, would think of this invitational asterisk. "It's right there in the Bible," Bruce told me on the way out. "Right in the Song of Solomon. *Your breasts are like twin fawns of a gazelle.*" Driving to meet a church member for lunch, I wondered if Bruce ever shared such a compliment with his wife, Harriet, who resembles a gazelle in many ways.

The following Tuesday, deviously, I asked Bruce if he had received much feedback from his book. Several female group members whispered quietly as we all turned to the book of Ephesians for that morning's study. "No, not even from my grandchildren," he said with a sad headshake, crestfallen that no one seemed to appreciate his noble efforts to educate and inform. I was always torn between wanting to slap Bruce for his annoying grandiosity and wanting to hug him because of his need for acceptance, which resembled the craving of a small child who never received enough parental affirmation.

Not long ago I met an interesting guy named Roland, who attends a church in Mountain Rest that observes what they call a "devil-stompin'" every fifth Sunday, a noisy and Spirit-filled attempt to drive Satan completely out of their midst and especially out of certain cantankerous members who "regularly behave like charismatic nincompoops," according to an elder in the congregation. The pastor is locally famous for sermons that regularly include this admonishment: "We're all gonna live forever! Don't y'all know that? Forever! But some of us in heaven and others of you in hell. Your choice, people!"

I doubt that their Satan-stomping would ever work with Lutherans, who've largely given up belief in organized evil—even though Brother Martin did throw that inkwell, famously, at the devil several centuries back while hiding out in Wartburg Castle in the Thuringian hill country. There's still a spot on the wall. I recall a long silence thirty-five years ago from my seminary theology professor, who listened to me ask if I "really had to invite parents to renounce Satan and all his empty promises" in the baptismal liturgy with such sweet little babies staring up at me. He let the question sink in for a while. I wasn't sure I believed in Satan at the time. "Spend twenty years in parish ministry and then come back and ask me this question again," he said. I haven't had to.

I met Roland in his Aunt Lucinda's backyard. My wife, Cindy, and I were pruning her box hedges for our annual "In as Much" community service weekend, based upon Jesus's instructions in Matthew 25. Roland introduced himself with a voice as gentle and sweet as the morning breeze that blew through Lucinda's yard. He is single, never married; a computer repair expert, immediately likeable.

I would never have picked Roland to attend a devil-stomping church, especially after he described in great detail his seven pet hermit crabs, each of whom responds to Roland's voice on cue with one of a half-dozen musical calls. His favorite crab, Captain Jack Sparrow, is deaf, not requiring a call, and rides around with Roland on daily errands, perched safely above the dashboard with antennae extended—even though he slipped out the passenger window once on a hard-left turn despite trying to frantically engage his claws in the cracked and fading automotive vinyl. Roland almost started to cry remembering that day. "We go real slow on the turns now." Then he brightened. "Would you like to meet Captain Jack? He's in the middle of his morning nap, but I doubt he would mind if we woke him up. He's a sweetheart."

Roland appeared at the box hedge a few minutes later, all smiles, cooing at the Captain and doing a little slow dance in half-circles. At one point he kissed his crab on the mouth with smooching sounds that freaked out Cindy just a bit. She says

I'm a magnet for lovable but certifiably odd people. "They're drawn to you for some reason. I will never understand it." All in a day's work for the Human Weathervane.

I'll miss people like Roland. There's something about being a minister that invites people to just be themselves and not hide their quirkiness. My grandmother, who lived over the mountain in Brevard, looked at me rather sternly just before she died while I was still in seminary. "You'll want to remember this," she said. "We're all a little cracked, actually."

Some of my favorite people in the congregation are two twin sisters, Candy and Sandy, who dress exactly the same each day, right down to their matching jewelry and cowboy boots. Once, when Candy went into the hospital with digestive challenges, I halfway expected Sandy to be wearing the same standard-issue hospital gown to help her sister feel right at home. "Have you ever had a church nightmare?" Sandy asked me once. I told her I had them all the time. "I keep dreaming," she said, "that we're at St. John's on Sunday morning, but we're not wearing the same clothes." I told the sisters about my pastor friends who dream about wearing no clothes at all in church. They got a big kick out of that.

It took me a while to tell the sisters apart. They are inseparable. I can't imagine what will happen when one of them dies. Both are married and maintain homes on opposite sides of town, but they choose to live all of each weekday in their childhood residence on Poplar Street near the church. I liked going by Candy and Sandy's when I needed a lift from a hard day. They both have great laughs and don't mind sharing just about any thought that comes to mind.

Candy loves animals and delights in painting various equine scenes of horses in action or repose, always in oil, with dozens of her efforts hanging around the house. "I wouldn't invite just anyone to come by and see this particular painting, pastor. But you are just the type of person to appreciate it." Across the room near the fireplace, Sandy twitters and softly claps her hands. "Oooh, sister, are you sure about showin' that one?"

Of course, I had to see it—Candy's painting of "my beautiful Indian princess whose bare chest is showin' astride a Palomino while her young lover kneels down near a creek in ad-my-ration." The painting wasn't half-bad. The young brave gazes with interest in understandable appreciation. I'm touched that Candy chose to share her art with the pastor.

On the way out, Candy shows me her glass curio containing about three hundred miniature horses she's collected over the years. I take a moment to admire them, like family to the sisters. Candy hesitates. "I know you're not going to believe this, but these two over here, right over on this side of the third shelf. They moved last night, all by themselves. This morning I found them over here. I think they want out." Free to run with the Indian Princess.

Just after I retired, the bishop made his annual visit to assist the congregation with the transition. I am told that the bishop went carefully through the clergy departure protocol and then asked for questions.

Bruce eagerly waved his hand. "I just want people to know that if they have any problem at all during the pastoral vacancy, they can come to me because I've been in so many leadership positions over the years—here's a list of them, if you want to see—that I doubt there's a single problem we may be facing that I won't be able to assist with." There were muffled groans, but Bruce didn't seem to notice.

I used to daydream about luring Bruce up to the clock tower at night, under the cover of darkness, near the weathervane, to ask him some obscure question about congregational history, maybe concerning the ancient process of hand-hewing the chestnut beams. Unfortunately, there's no space in the tower for a Poe-like Amontillado room where I can secretly stow Bruce and save the future pastor a lot of headaches.

Lacking a place to seal him away, I imagine asking Bruce to help me examine the stuck minute hand on the outside clock face, since I understand he's had lots of experience as a watchmaker in his youth. When he leans out the window to examine the clock, I give him a little push, privately reconciling the action with a conviction that he is indeed Jesus-like and probably wants to "jump off the pinnacle of the temple" to reveal authentic messianic tendencies once and for all. Just the merest of pushes, and Bruce would be lying down in the green grass below. I could even point him toward the post office.

Forgive these dark daydreams. But all pastors have them. You know that by now.

Embrace Your Role as the Human Weathervane

Sermons don't occur in a vacuum. They occur with very real people whose joys, sufferings, questions, annoying habits, infidelities, voting proclivities, gossip, sacrifice, glaring sins, faithfulness, and hearts for community service make up the diverse and sometimes-maddening body known as a congregation. And, to top it off, they've called a sinner with some of the same personality traits to be their pastor.

As a sermon theme begins to take shape—usually by Wednesday, if you've been attentive to the disciplines described earlier in the week—it is vitally important to bring into your imagination the specific people who will eventually hear the Word forming in your pastoral heart and soul. Churches are filled with some of the best people you'd ever want to meet, and also some of the most annoying. This is undoubtedly testimony to the creative power of the Spirit and the timeless message of a man who once said, "And I, when I am lifted up from the earth, will draw all people to myself" (John 12:32). This is a wonderfully inclusive statement, but one that can test a pastor's patience when enacted practically on the congregational level. If "all" people are drawn, chances are that some of them will be difficult.

Like a weathervane, pastors listen for the wind of the Spirit and point with the sermon in that direction, using the sermon to bring healing and health. Preaching, therefore, is often difficult (and sometimes unpopular) work. Recall Saint Paul's provocative question posed to one congregation of his acquaintance: "Have I now become your enemy by telling you the truth?" (Gal. 4:16).

Early in my pastoral career, I once thought that many parishioners didn't spend much time reading the Bible because of various time-crunches involving vocation and family. I have since concluded that this isn't the primary reason for infrequent Scripture reading. The Bible means to change us. Conversion to Christ is often a painfully jarring enterprise.

The sermon will explore the radical love of God that draws us all together in Christ, *and* the sanctifying work of the Holy Spirit, who intends to shape us all into his likeness, "until all of us come to the unity of the faith and of the knowledge of the Son of God, to maturity, to the measure of the full stature of Christ" (Eph. 4:13). Read this verse again, slowly. It shouldn't surprise pastors that many people actively connected to a congregation still aren't ready (consciously or unconsciously) to sign on for such a project, which results in theological maturity resembling that of Christ.

One of the tasks of the sermon, therefore, must include the goal of spiritual formation in a land where all of us are exposed to vast amounts of misinformation, much of it alarming and some of it useless. In a recent issue of *The Atlantic*, Kurt Andersen describes several of our nation's rather odd beliefs:

> A third of us believe not only that global warming is no big deal but that it is a hoax perpetrated by scientists, the government, and journalists. A third believe that our earliest ancestors were humans just like us; that the government has, in league with the pharmaceutical industry, hidden evidence of natural cancer cures; that extraterrestrials have visited or are visiting Earth. Almost a quarter believe that vaccines cause autism, and that Donald Trump won the popular vote in 2016. A quarter believe that our previous president maybe or definitely was (or is?) the anti-Christ. According to a survey by Public Policy Polling, 15 percent believe that the "media or the government adds secret mind-controlling technology to television broadcast signals," and another 15 percent think that is possible. A quarter of Americans believe in witches . . . the same proportion that believes U.S. officials were complicit in the 9/11 attacks.[2]

Certainly (hopefully) these statistics are different in the congregation where you are currently a pastor. My point in citing them here is that all of us are potentially shaped by vast gobs of information streamed into our households in a way unprecedented in human history. We are a skeptical people, vulnerable to whacky theories and convictions that undeniably spill into congregational life and shape the minds and hearts of at least some of our church members. "Christian spiritual formation," writes Sally Brown, "is actually a process of *counterformation*. Sermons are more likely to fulfill their potential as counterformative discourse if the preacher acquaints himself or herself with the sort of sociocultural formation that shapes the consciousness of those in the pews."[3]

It is important for a pastor to quietly probe (in meetings, during visits at hospital bedsides, over lunch) not only *that* parishioners hold certain beliefs, but also *how* an individual may have arrived at such beliefs. A reason usually exists. Quietly attempt to discover the reason. There is a pastoral art to listening to another human being without judgment. It isn't the pastor's job (via a winning personality and scripted erudition) to convince a parishioner of a more enlightened position on a variety of pressing topics. Conversion is ultimately part of Christ's job description, working through the Holy Spirit. Again, recall the weathervane. We point in the direction of the Spirit's revelations in Scripture. When questioned (and all faithful pastors are questioned[4]), it is appropriate to note that we aren't making up God's word as we go. I've had people leave the church over certain sermons I've preached. In most instances (though not all, I confess), I have attempted to have a conversation with them about the nature of the Bible and the particular text that raised their ire. Speaking the truth in love is never an easy enterprise and may serve to exacerbate the divide rather than mend it. But an attempt at reconciliation at least tries to model Jesus's attempts at discourse with those who disagreed with him.

Befriend the Skeptic

Speaking of skepticism, examined from another angle, I have found my atheist and agnostic friends, rather ironically, to be very helpful preaching allies. Their long friendships serve as a safe context for honest give-and-take that has sharpened my openness to converse with someone holding a different viewpoint without the covert agenda of trying to talk the conversation partner into something.

My good friend Andy lives alone on thirty acres of land in central Maine near the Kennebec River with a couple of dogs and no electricity or indoor plumbing. He's hiked the Appalachian Trail in its entirety five separate times, not to mention the Continental Divide and Pacific Crest Trails once each. If you do the math, that's about 15,000 miles of wilderness hiking. He has to snowshoe two miles in the winter months to get to his parked truck. He loves the land and loves the solitude; he loves the hard work required for such a solitary existence.

Andy and I have written long letters back and forth for forty years, always about some aspect of why I believe in God and he doesn't. We met at a lakeside camp for mentally challenged youth and adults. I recall sitting on the floor of a cabin at three AM with Andy as I rocked a very troubled child in my arms whose fits of flailing would hurt himself and others in his cabin. The night finally became quiet except for the noise of crickets outside. "If we give God thanks for sunsets," Andy finally asked, "shouldn't we also praise the Lord for hurricanes?" It wasn't hard to decipher his meaning.

My path to seminary culminated in a first year after which I was fairly sure I wasn't going to stay. I occasionally sat under the pecan trees during Morning Prayer, writing letters to Andy. "Quit skipping chapel, you son of a bitch," he wrote back.

Now that I've been a pastor in a variety of interesting settings, it's rather odd for me to look back and admit that an atheist has been one of my theological companions for four decades, a friend who once told me that if God did appear to him one fine day, he would "chase him down the path with a pitchfork." We have exchanged hundreds of letters. And his questions about suffering and God's omnipotence have pushed me to articulate difficult responses better than any theology class I have ever taken.

My pastoral writing interests have taken clear shape because of Andy. I am passionate about the historic catechumenate, offering candidates a protracted catechetical process prior to baptism, convinced that the "express conversion" practiced in many churches helps neither the convert nor the congregation. Newcomers to the faith need plenty of time to ask questions and ponder the cost of discipleship. Oddly, Andy taught me over the years that a quick baptismal splash into the arms of God is possibly not authentic, given the rather strange life into which Jesus invites followers.

One of the towns where I lived for fourteen years—Abingdon, Virginia—is filled with artists, craftspeople, and lots of atheists and agnostics. My doctoral work (which became a book)[5] centered on how two different groups of local residents heard and processed typical Sunday sermons. One group consisted of fifteen convinced skeptics whom I'd come to know at parties and other gatherings. The other group was made up of folk returning to church after a long absence—most of their adult lives. An attorney in the first group described himself as a "Frisbeetarian," playfully explaining that his soul would float up on the roof at his death, and no one could get it down.

From these two groups I learned a lot about preaching and Christian communication and how outsiders and new-comers heard and processed Sunday proclamation within a liturgical context. I'm fairly sure that my friendship with Andy (and maintaining a non-defensive posture about my identity as a Christian pastor) opened lots of doors in that community.

A couple of years ago I took my young adult son, Lukas, on a road trip to Maine to visit Andy. Although the letter connection remained strong, neither of us had seen him in many years. (Lukas was a little boy the last time he saw Andy.) We took the interstate up through Vermont, followed a two-lane for many miles, came to the end of a rural road, and kept going. We got lost. I was beginning to think we'd have to spend the night in the car with the local moose as our companions. In the last light of day, we finally found the house and a diminutive man waiting for us. We talked and laughed into the night on Andy's front porch in the Maine woods.

I suppose there are a limited number of ministerial paths a pastor might take upon leaving seminary. We are formed by Sunday school teachers, theology professors, CPE, and internship supervisors. But my journey has also been centrally shaped by a leprechaun of a man who doesn't believe in God. When I told him recently about my newest publication, he said, "Oh, goody—another book about the Lord."

Invest time in unhurried conversations with a variety of people, inside the church and outside, who will teach you how to listen for how they arrived at certain convictions, and along the way will invite you to articulate what you believe and how you came to believe it. These conversations will powerfully shape the themes that surface in any preaching text and the words you choose for proclamation. Again, take the Bible lection for your Sunday sermon with you into these conversations, even if you never refer to it.

Become a Scriptural Sleuth

By now, I hope that you've noticed my near-obsession with taking notes (not necessarily from the commentaries) on lectionary texts in various out-of-the-way locales. Inspiration for a sermon can occur anywhere, and a preacher must be ready. The novice preacher will need to develop some sort of system to record ideas, jottings from unexpected brainstorms, snippets of conversation, intersections from the news, observations of various human interactions, and odd images from dreams. This doesn't mean you'll use everything you record, but save your notes. You may find a new theme in old notes when the same texts roll around again three years from now.

Developing a system for taking notes and gathering illustrative material sharpen a preacher's budding inclination to take every word of Scripture seriously. I waste words all the time in chatter, gossip, anger, and feckless frivolity. God indulges distracted and weary pastors like me to a point. But let your hermeneutical assumption be that there are no throwaway words in the Bible. Every word and nuance counts.

Learning how to see God's word angularly takes time in a process that's really never finished. My friend Tom Long explains this well:

> Sometimes people assume that preaching works this way: a preacher prepares a sermon during the week, finishes it at some point—maybe Friday afternoon or Saturday night—and then gets up and preaches the finished product in worship on Sunday. This may be the way it appears on the surface, but experienced preachers know better; sermons are actually never finished. There are always loose ends, questions that could have been pursued in more depth, stones left unturned, intriguing aspects of the biblical text left unexamined, thoughts not quite fully baked, an untidiness at the heart of things. At some point, though, preachers have to take what they have, stand up, and speak. *Preachers do not preach because the sermon is finished; they preach because it is Sunday. The time has come.*[6]

Bible texts are similar to ordinary people in that there's always more than meets the eye at first glance. Part of a pastor's care of souls in the parish involves attempting to look beyond certain personality traits and patiently working to discover *why* a particularly difficult person behaves the way they do. (Even with someone like Bruce, mentioned earlier in this chapter.) As a preacher devises a strategy to address a group of complex individuals (including the complex preacher), the sermon process dares not shelve the pastoral task of corporate congregational exegesis with the multilayered people (some of whose layers are carefully hidden) whom God has called us to lead toward ongoing conversion.

Similarly, any biblical text will also be endlessly revelatory to the careful eye and ear of a seasoned pastor. "Indeed, the word of God is living and active, sharper than any two-edged sword, piercing until it divides soul from spirit, joints from marrow; it is able to judge the thoughts and intentions of the heart" (Heb. 4:12). Martin Luther once likened preaching to surgery. The surgical process can heal, but also inevitably brings discomfort along the way via unwelcome probing. Assuming that this amazing claim from Hebrews is true and spiritually accurate, it behooves the preacher to include "investigative scriptural sleuth" as a central part of the pastoral job description in a fashion no less carefully meticulous than a surgeon's.

I like to think of the four friends who presumably climbed a ladder while bearing a stretcher (Mark 2:1–4). They persistently dug through the roof in order to lower their palsied friend down to Jesus, who was undoubtedly pleased with the effort and the new skylight and even the dirt collecting on the coffee table. To what lengths is a preacher willing to "dig" in leading a congregation to gospel truth in a text that may carry multiple insights and truths?

By way of illustration, wade with me into the delightfully deep waters of an old text with multiple layers that are not obvious at a quick glance: the healing of Naaman in 2 Kings 5:1–14, a story known by Jesus and used in one of his early sermons (see Luke 4:27) to stretch local perception of the wideness of God's love.

Full disclosure: Elisha the prophet is among my all-time favorite characters in the Bible. Once, when an ax-head was accidentally dropped into the Jordan, he made it float (2 Kings 6:7). The hiker in me loves that story. Elisha also had this cool trick of intercepting military messages telepathically (6:12), a gift that infuriated the Aramean opposition. He once purified a rancid pot of stew (4:40–41) that was making people sick, and also raised a boy from the dead (4:35) who then proceeded to sneeze, curiously, seven straight times just before opening his eyes.

Elisha was once called "baldy" by a group of rowdy boys (2:23). The prophet (perhaps having a bad hair day) summoned from the woods two angry she-bears, who then proceeded to maul forty-two of the children. Somewhere in my files I have a rather peculiar woodcut depicting a grinning she-bear with a large paw on the neck of one of the impertinent boys.

But my favorite story about Elisha involves Naaman, the furious and leprous commander of the army of the King of Aram. The Arameans were sworn enemies of the children of Israel, but this story drops in the weird little detail (5:1) that God once used Naaman's military skills to give victory over God's own people. God used a foreigner to rough up the chosen ones. God does this several times in the Bible—uses a so-called enemy to teach the chosen people a thing or two, revealing to the careful pastor/scribe that no nation can pretend to have the Lord tucked away safely in its blessed back pocket in a "God Bless America" (but no one else) perception of the divine. The Bible is a book that candidly confesses that God is also up to divine business with other nations.[7]

File this detail away in a Wednesday note. And now back to Naaman, a proud, decorated field marshal who has everything going for him—medals, money, his picture on the front page of *The Aram Free Press*. He has it all, except for one little thing. Naaman is a leper, and it bugs the dickens out of him, far more than any pedestrian eczema, seborrhea, or signs of psoriasis. One day Naaman is complaining about his symptoms to his Israelite–P.O.W. slave girl. "You know," she says, "I remember this guy back home in Israel who can maybe help you." With the permission of the king and well before the days of Blue Cross–Blue Shield, Naaman sets out on a long, dusty journey in search of this foreign health-care provider.

A careful preacher/scribe will note this also: Naaman loads up a huge pile of glittering loot to butter up the prophet. A single talent of silver weighs seventy-five pounds.[8] Naaman comes booming up to the healer's door with 750 pounds of silver, a wagon-load of glittering gold, and ten of the best sports coats that money can buy. It's an absurd amount of stuff for a prophet who doesn't have a whole lot hanging in his closet. But this reveals a lot about Naaman. He is an "entitled" man. He is a guy used to getting his way and becoming loud when he doesn't.

So, see the picture here. Naaman comes rolling up to Elisha's front door, full of military pride, pompous faith in his own credentials, and a health problem that needs fixing. It doesn't say so in the text, but I get the distinct feeling that Naaman is expecting people to jump when he says "jump." In one of my former parishes, there was an older man who had the annoying habit of swinging by the parsonage early in the morning, pulling up in the driveway, and honking the horn until somebody came out to see what he wanted. I loved this man, but he was undeniably a guy used to getting his own way and throwing around his considerable power in town.

Elisha (as you have now meticulously noticed from his own resumé) was a prophet consistently unimpressed by the relative power of human beings. Elisha worked for God. Elisha knew about real power. That's why, when Naaman honks his horn (so to speak) in front of Elisha's parsonage door, the prophet doesn't even bother to come outside. He sends his prophetic Rx—the watery prescription for the cure of leprosy—by a messenger. This, please note, absolutely sends Naaman through the roof. "I thought that for me (for *me*, after all), he would surely come out and at least wave his hand and say a few magic words" (5:11). *Does he know who I am? Don't we have rivers back home that are far more glorious than this mudhole?*

Perhaps it's easy to notice the parody of proud Naaman in this old story. Watch him throw a little temper tantrum beside the road. Notice him hopping up and down in a proud fit. It takes a while to learn how to read the Bible faithfully. It's a sneaky book. We read these old stories of leprosy and healing of one affliction or another. But if we read them too quickly, we'll miss their power. Naaman got better because he followed Elisha's prescription. I love the image of the proud, decorated general dipping his rear end in the muddy Jordan seven times. He went home a healed and happy man.

But a preacher has to wonder. Was leprosy Naaman's main problem? It was certainly his *stated* problem. The story suggests it was driving him crazy. But I have to think that Elisha (and God) knew about a far more serious problem—an "inner leprosy" in Naaman's life that was full of pride, arrogance, anger, entitlement, and snap judgments. Humility is a tough thing to teach. God can't wiggle the divine nose and instantly make people humble. Learning humility may be a far larger project than curing leprosy.

Part of what this old story teaches is that God often doesn't act in the way we choose to summon him. God is often after bigger fish to fry in our lives, which may require time, patience, and a prescription that can't be filled overnight and according to personal whim.

I've taken some time with this old story to reveal its rather angular truths (not obvious at first glance) that surface in taking seriously the narrative's many details, dropped by the author of Second Kings like bits of bread along a path. Coupling the exegetical (and sometimes playful) insights from a Bible text with the ongoing exegesis of congregational life in one's first call after seminary, a new preacher will fill several pages with notes for a possible sermon. How pastors listen to others invariably shapes how pastors will listen to texts. Thursday's tasks will now center on distilling your notes of observation into a faithful theme that will direct Friday's writing.

4
THURSDAY

Naming

Liberate the Sermon's Purpose

There's an amusing scene in *To Kill a Mockingbird* where Jem and Scout attend church one Sunday with their beloved housekeeper, Calpurnia, at the First Purchase A.M.E Church in the Quarters. Scout narrates the experience:

> Reverend Sykes used his pulpit more freely to express his views on individual lapses from grace: Jim Hardy had been absent from church for five Sundays and he wasn't sick; Constance Jackson had better watch her ways—she was in grave danger for quarreling with her neighbors. . . . One by one, the congregation came forward and dropped nickels and dimes into a black enameled coffee can. . . . To our amazement, Reverend Sykes emptied the can onto the table and raked the coins into his hand. He straightened up and said, "This is not enough. . . ." Reverend Sykes waved his hand and called to someone in the back of the church. "Alec, shut the doors. Nobody leaves here till we have ten dollars."[1]

I suspect most pastors love this scene and daydream darkly of the Sunday where names of the uncommitted are revealed during the announcement period and slack stewardship is publicly exposed from the pulpit for all to discover. I have a friend who recalls a worship service from his childhood where the priest intoned, "Now take the William Murphy family, for instance. They take in eighty grand annually and give a measly forty dollars a year to the church!" That, of course, was the last the congregation ever saw of the Murphy family.

My gleeful parishioner-exposure daydreams are dampened as I encounter more and more people who self-describe as "recovering Christians," people still getting over an emotionally abusive religious adolescence or young adulthood. I meet recovering Christians at parties, at schools, and in hospital elevators. A woman recently told me, "I had so much religion and God crammed into my head as a child—with so much fear and manipulation and weekly threat—that I will never set foot in a church building again as long as I live." Short of some Damascus Road-like encounter, I believe her.

I saw a road sign in the North Carolina Mountains a few years ago that read "Jesus or Hell." Just those three words. I'm thankful and honored when I meet someone who trusts me enough to share their story about a past filled with religious trauma, but also rather sad because such stories are rather common but so far from my own experience.

Because of my parents' divergent vocational and political viewpoints, we talked about all sorts of things at the Honeycutt dinner table when my brothers and I were young—politics, sports, religion, the crazy neighbors. (Ever notice how it's always the *neighbors* who are deemed unbalanced?) And I know these dinner talks shaped my perceptions of church and God and my calling as a pastor. But as I meet more and more people who are largely "done" with religion, I realize that my childhood dinner talks with parents who got me to think are perhaps rare.

There's much more childhood religious manipulation in people we encounter than pastors often realize. We sometimes miss the unspoken suspicion in the minds of many people who may assume that all clergy are out to instill guilt and kidnap minds. Our recognition of and response to such early coercion in a person's life may be the most important things we do to help him or her revisit any possibility of God or church.

Jesus rarely tries to pound the truth of something into people, an important observation for new preachers moving toward the Thursday "naming" of a sermon theme. The very first words out of Jesus's mouth in John's Gospel (1:38) come in the form of a question: *What are you looking for?* This old question certainly invites a search for something more profound than our car keys, but hardly suggests anything resembling manipulative threat. Jesus never tries to hammer home truth coercively. "If any *want* to become my followers, let them deny themselves and take up their cross and follow me" (Mark 8:34, my italics). There is specificity with the invitation, but no coercion.

And there can be no arm-twisting in authentic Sunday proclamation. Jesus teases and coaxes the truth to the surface from a very old well. "Sermons," writes Fred Craddock, "should proceed or move in such a way as to give the listener something to think, feel, decide, and do during the preaching. It is a poor division of labor that assigns the sermon totally to the preacher and the post-sermon 'go and do' to the listener."[2]

Jesus seems much more concerned about theological depth than numerical success in his preaching and teaching. Recall the five thousand people drawn to Jesus during the multiplication of a little boy's little lunch. After Jesus expands on the sacramental meaning of this meal, people leave his entourage in droves. "Because of this many of his disciples turned back and no longer went about with him" (John 6:66). Jesus, however, doesn't seem at all bothered by this departure.

There is a delicate balance in preaching between avoiding coercion and being honest about the radical call to discipleship. Two rather pointed questions posed by Jesus from this same section of John particularly stand out as I think about sharing the gospel with those who've given up on church due to a negative experience in the past. (Both questions are important to keep in mind as you tackle the Thursday task of naming your sermon theme.) You will encounter such people while making community rounds in your first parish; and more people in this category than you might think will appear in church pews to "check out the new pastor" after a long absence from congregational life.

First question: *Does this offend you?* (John 6:61). Well, of course it does. The teachings of Jesus can be completely offensive. Unlike me at times, Jesus isn't interested in pleasing everybody. His ideas about the reign of God and the inclusion of the least, last, and lost are inherently offensive. If a congregation isn't occasionally offended by Jesus, then I'd have to wonder if they were engaging in selective listening. *Of course we're offended by Jesus!* He means to change us and help us live life from odd angles. Spiritual offense is an important component of any authentic conversion process in the Christian life.

But spiritual offense is always different from religious manipulation, and different from past religious coercion that's so emotionally damaging to people who've given up on church. Jesus says, "I have told you that no one can come to me unless it is granted by the Father" (John 6:65). Think about this statement that occurs between the two questions I'm highlighting here. If this statement is true, why would a religious community even bother with emotional coercion and turning up the heat? Jesus wasn't about pushing people. Authentic discipleship is more about feeling drawn, not being pushed.

In Miriam Toews's wonderful novel set in a small town in Manitoba, a teenager named Nomi, the story's narrator, describes her reading habits and how she feels utterly trapped in her censorial church community:

> I am not a fan of fantasy. There's so much of that being crammed down our throats every day in this place. The mark of the beast? Streets paved in gold? Seven white horses? . . . I dream of escaping into the *real* world. If I am forced to read one more Narnia series book I will kill myself. I would love to read the diary of a girl my age—a girl from the city. Or a textbook on urban planning. Or a New York City phone book. I would kill to own a New York City phone book.[3]

Perhaps pastors need to develop a rite of theological recovery (or at least a rite of doubting, an option alongside the rite of welcome) to address people in our churches who have backgrounds even harsher than Nomi's.

There's a second question posed by Jesus in proximity to the first. People are leaving in droves. Jesus looks around and sees that his popularity has dwindled from five thousand to twelve. But as people are heading for the exits, Jesus slowly turns to the inner circle, his closest friends, and dares to ask, *Do you also wish to go away?* (John 6:67). Simon Peter has an excellent and famous answer to this question, of course. Jesus does indeed have the words of eternal life. But I fear we tend to move on from this second question too quickly. Jesus is pretty much telling his closest followers that it's okay to depart if they feel uncomfortable.

I recall a young man named Brian who came to our church several years ago seeking baptism. He entered a catechumenal group that would help him prepare for the sacrament at Easter. After several weeks spent in reflection, reading, common prayer, and conversation, Brian came to the group meeting one Wednesday evening and announced he no longer wanted to be baptized. The group talked that night about his desire to leave and agreed to meet the following week to see if Brian had perhaps changed his mind. He returned the following Wednesday with a clear and definite decision not to be baptized. We prayed with Brian and then watched him walk out into the night. After his departure, a couple of the group members were in tears. They had come to love and care for Brian. I was proud of them for listening to his reasons and receiving his brave decision without judgment. There can be no evangelical arm-twisting, however subtle, within any authentic Christian community.

Any pastor can occasionally look out on Sunday mornings and notice that some people are present under duress. It's clear they don't want to be in church. Maybe a spouse turned up the heat. Maybe a family obligation dragged them to worship. I wish I'd sometimes had the caring wherewithal to leave my perch, wander out among the pews, place my hand on a shoulder, and say, "It's okay. It's really okay; you can leave if you want to."

There is indeed truthful honesty about the theological depth expected by Jesus; there's no getting around that. But the man twists the arm of no one who opts out entirely from his kingdom enterprise. When a preacher truly believes this— that the aim of preaching is not to raise money, cheerlead for a pet project, increase Sunday-morning attendance, or manipulate the lost into a forced decision—new possibilities open up for the sermon's purpose and direction.

Depending on the Jesus one may have grown up with, these two questions may scramble one's God game-board and shape a variety of compelling sermon themes. Jesus can indeed be offensive, but there is no coercion here, and there are no hellish threats, even in a rather graphic story he tells about hell.

Refuse Hellish Manipulation

All major world religions have some sort of theology, tradition, or vivid folklore concerning the fate of just and unjust people in the afterlife. In the Bible, however, both hell and heaven get only a handful of descriptive scenes concerning their respective geographies, furniture, and residents of the neighborhood.

But through the centuries, hell has captured the moral imagination of the church much more than heaven. Religious folk have needed a place to send wayward people. For many, motivation for living a moral life still resides in hell-avoidance. A parishioner once asked me, "If there's no hell waiting on bad people, Pastor Frank, then why bother with doing the right thing?"

Presumably we need a place to send our enemies. Someone once wryly noted that the only thing that might eclipse the satisfaction of *knowing* an enemy is in hell is to actually *see* them there. "One of the less savory notions of the early Church," writes Alice Turner, "was that of *abominable fancy*, the idea that part of the joy of the saved lay in contemplating the tortures of the damned. In many illustrations, blessed souls, arranged in orderly rows, their eyes lowered demurely toward the fiery chaos beneath, watch heaven's eternal late-night TV."[4] The story of the rich man and Lazarus (Luke 16:19–31) seems to suggest such a possibility.

Scores of religious paintings from the Middle Ages, when few were literate, graphically depict the fate of the damned. Lazarus in Abraham's "bosom" virtually litters the artistic landscape for centuries in a variety of countries. Down below is the unfortunate rich man, popularly known as Dives, begging for just a drop of cool water. Request denied.

Old sermons on this old story frequently tip-toed up to (and often crossed) the line of moral extortion.[5] Many Christians no longer believe in the fiery hell assumed by so many of the faithful for so long. Interestingly, our national desire for revenge—often masquerading under the word "justice"—has risen in the last fifty years at the same time our belief in hell has waned. For if there is no hell, we'd better punish infidels now, while there's still time, while they're still breathing—and in doing so we're taking justice once assigned to God alone into our own hands. Though Americans may largely disbelieve in hell, our national behaviors often suggest that we also disbelieve in God, the ultimate judge who allows time for repentance and change, even in the lives of those who've made horrible mistakes.

In January of 1985, I attended a late-evening rally protesting the execution of a South Carolina man on death row. Two opposing groups of people waited in vigil outside the state prison. When news of the inmate's death via electric chair was announced, those in favor of the execution broke into cheers, wild applause, and a recurring chant: "The sucker fried!" In a landscape without God, the thirst for revenge on this side of the grave undeniably spikes.

The story from Luke 16 raises a large question for pastors who write and deliver sermons: *How do people change?* How does this fabulously wealthy man who had a penchant for purple part with some of his wealth to help a man he walked by and ignored every day? How does he begin to see the poor at his gate?

I guess what I'm asking is this: *What is the purpose of this parable?* Do Christians support various relief organizations that assist the hungry because God will get us if we don't? That has certainly been the classic and dominant interpretation of this story. The thinking goes something like this: If fear has caused someone to think twice about helping the poor (clearly friends of Jesus), then maybe homiletical manipulation isn't all bad.

I find it fascinating, though, that this very parable that seems to be all about hell ultimately refuses threats and graphic warnings to get the greedy to become generous. In other words, Jesus refrains from using hell to scare the hell out of people. If God were truly serious about getting people to change by means of fear tactics and moral manipulation, *why not* send Lazarus back to warn the rest of the rich man's family with an agenda similar to that of the three ghosts who awaken miserly Ebenezer Scrooge in the classic Dickens tale?

But Abraham won't agree to this. He won't agree to use threats or coercive warnings. His answer is telling: "Your family will not be convinced even if someone rises from the dead." Which is why you'll never see Jesus make a guest appearance on a game show or on *Jimmy Kimmel Live!*, trying to prove his existence and convince people to change. According to this parable, neither the threat of hell nor the promise of heaven is going to truly change people. So, let me return to the question: What will?

Abraham replies to the wealthy man concerning his brothers (and to us across the centuries): "They have Moses and the prophets; they should listen to them" (16:29). And that's all the advice (or warning) that Father Abraham will offer from the other side of the grave.

Humans aren't born knowing how to live a meaningful life. But neither can we be scolded or harangued *into* such a life. We must be formed, reborn—the church's primary mission and essence, according to Matthew 28:18–20. "Christians are made, not born," early church apologist Tertullian (155–240 CE) wisely observed.

Listening to the old stories and finding our story in them is how we change. The church proclaims that God is so consistently on the side of the poor that Christ's disciples must be too, or else we run the risk of living outside the story.

"I am thoroughly convinced," writes Dallas Willard, "that God will let everyone into heaven who, in his considered opinion, can stand it. But 'standing it' may prove to be a more difficult matter than those who take their view of heaven from popular movies or popular preaching may think. The fires in heaven may be hotter than those in the other place."[6] Our habits and disciplines as Christ's followers in this life prepare us for life with him in the next. Perhaps Christ's "judgment" is based less on a system of reward and punishment and more on a perception of whether a person is joyfully willing to enter into the realities of heaven.[7]

Perhaps hell is a life lived willfully and consistently with self at the center while the radical inclusion taught by Jesus in the beloved community remains at the periphery. The Apostles' Creed reports that Jesus, after his crucifixion, even "descended into hell," presumably looking for people who reside there. He gives up on no one with the invitation, but he also coerces no one.

Develop a Theme Statement

By Thursday at the latest, a sermon's direction should be guided by a single theme statement authored by the Spirit's nudges in the various textual brainstorms you've recorded after prayer, the notes from personal encounters, the insights from questions you've brought to the commentaries, and the random jottings at stoplights. But this is more difficult than it might at first seem, according to Fred Craddock:

> Most preachers confess to having difficulty stating the message in one simple sentence. For some the difficulty lies in the fact that the discipline here involves decision, not only about what will be said but also about what will not be said. To say one thing is to decide not to say something else. It is

to accept the conclusion that on any given Sunday, many wonderful Christian things will not be said.[8]

Remember that your listeners will appreciate thematic focus. Like it or not, pastors must concede that listening to someone speak for fifteen minutes straight is becoming a lost and challenging discipline for many parishioners saturated with various and compelling electronic media that don't require sustained concentration, partly because the information can be retrieved later with a simple mouse-click.

The faithful at Jerusalem's ancient Water Gate (see Nehemiah 8:1–12)—ears attuned not long after the exile to the echoes of the mistakes of their forebears—listened with rapt attention from early morning until midday to public reading "from the book, from the law of God, with interpretation" (8:8). Try eight hours of Scripture reading and preaching today in your congregation to discover how to clear a church building quickly.

Neil Postman (1931–2003) illustrates how American listening skills have eroded in our country's history by citing the length of the Lincoln-Douglas debates that commenced in August of 1858 in Ottawa, Illinois. "Their arrangement provided that Douglas would speak first, for one hour; Lincoln would take an hour and a half to reply; Douglas, a half hour to rebut Lincoln's reply."[9] Postman adds that the 1858 exchange between the two men was preceded by far lengthier encounters. He cites a Peoria debate in October of 1854 that lasted seven hours. The questions Postman poses are noteworthy:

> What kind of audience was this? Who were these people who could so cheerfully accommodate themselves to seven hours of oratory? . . . For one thing, its attention span

would obviously have been extraordinary by current standards. Is there any audience of Americans today who could endure seven hours of talk? or five? or three? Especially without pictures of any kind? Second, these audiences must have had an equally extraordinary capacity to comprehend lengthy and complex sentences aurally. In Douglas' Ottawa speech he included in his one-hour address three long, legally phrased resolutions of the Abolition platform. Lincoln, in his reply, read even longer passages from a published speech he had delivered on a previous occasion. . . . It is hard to imagine the present occupant of the White House being capable of constructing such clauses in similar circumstances. And if he were, he would surely do so at the risk of burdening the comprehension or concentration of his audience.[10]

These words were written in 1985. If my wife (a high-school English teacher) is a reliable witness, the erosion of attention to the spoken word in the thirty-plus years since has only gotten worse. A tightly worded theme statement that serves as gatekeeper for a particular Sunday's homiletic content may be the single most important component in a preacher's sermon planning and decision-making. I'll come back to the necessity of editing a sermon in the next chapter. For now, it's enough to say that the theme statement will guard against excess and distracting clutter in the sermon. Review one by one the cornucopia of insightful gems you've faithfully recorded over the last few days. The theme statement will determine whether their moment is now or later.

The theme statement should be worded as simply as possible so that the preacher may return to it throughout the sermon much like a fiction writer returns to a controlling meta-phor in a short story. This doesn't mean the theme statement need be repeated many times (or even once) for the sermon's duration, but a listener should be able to state specifically, upon departing worship, what the sermon was indeed about.

I preached the following sermon (based upon Luke 21:5–19) on November 13, 2016, the Sunday following a very con-tentious and divisive presidential election. I offer it here not as a model of sterling homiletical success, but as an example of how a theme statement directs and shapes the sermon. Read the sermon, let it sit a minute, and then try writing a short, one-sentence theme for this particular piece of proclamation.

I Will Give You Words

". . . for I will give you words and a wisdom . . ." (Luke 21:15)

Here on this Sunday morning after Election Day, I suspect some of you are elated, and some of you are depressed. Our voting proclivi-ties even here at little old Saint John's undoubtedly vary. I am not a Facebook follower, but I have heard about various church-member posts on both sides of the aisle, so I am reasonably sure the emo-tions in this room this morning, at least politically speaking, are mixed. People are "de-friending" each other, I am told. And even though I am not completely sure what that really implies, social me-dia dropout that I am, it sounds rather alarming to this old pastor.

We say in the Pledge that we are "indivisible," and I think most people truly believe that; at least I hope we do. But we are a very splintered and divided nation these days in about any way you can name. President-elect Trump will have his hands full, as did

President Obama and others before them. And you might say that we have always had differences of opinion as a nation, and you would be correct. But I think we have entered another era entirely in this regard.

Emotions run high at election time. We think "our" candidate (whoever that might be) will emerge and solve all our problems. We are news junkies at this time of the year, and we hope that someone (anyone) will step in and steer the country in a preferred direction. We assign unrealistic (and probably unattainable) expectations to candidates who are human and flawed and fallible, just like us.

Into this rather loud din of shouts and accusations, for Christians anyway, steps the man Jesus, who (please recall) has risen from the dead and presumably reigns in our lives as Lord — a rather jarring and descriptive word that basically means "Head-Guy-In-Charge-Of-Our-Lives-As-We-Face-Any-And-All-Decisions." He is not just a great man from the past, like some *uber*-Abraham Lincoln. He's alive and loose in the world, leading us. At least I hope that is true for you.

I always have to check myself during national elections to see who I am truly listening *to*. I am not affiliated with any particular party (and never will be), but I read widely and listen and talk and gossip about candidates and probably even spread rumors and act like I know what I am talking about and then suddenly realize that I am completely caught up in the din and realize I have just spent an entire day immersed in opinion and argument and worry . . . with Jesus on the sidelines, patiently waiting for me to get around to consulting him. Just for grins this week, do a serious inventory of your time. Add up the minutes (hours?) that you've spent with your favorite newspaper or TV news source or talk-radio host. And then honestly examine the time you've spent in consulting Jesus in the Bible or via prayer. And if you are like me, you may be shamed by this exercise.

Yes, we are a divided nation. And that undoubtedly means we are a divided church. But Christians do have this man in common, right? And whether your emotions are high or low this morning, I hope we can confess that our Savior is not elected in a voting booth. He has no term limits. He's been appointed by God to lead us. It behooves us, then, to consult him and look to him in all times and places—more (decidedly more) than *any* president of this nation. If this is not consistently true of this or any church, then God help us.

* * *

We are only two Sundays from the beginning of Advent, and here at the end of the church year Jesus is giving a little nostalgia tour of the temple in Jerusalem. This place of worship and pilgrimage was an impressive architectural wonder in its day, rivaling any Trump Tower in resultant awe and admiration. Jesus got lost there when he was twelve, and his worried parents found the prescient lad impressing even those who ran the place. Jesus laments over Jerusalem from a hill a few chapters before this one in Luke. He called out to people to come under his sheltering wisdom, but they would not listen. The temple was undoubtedly in view as he lamented over a city he loved.

The words this morning from the temple tour guide are rather jarring. The disciples are agog at the beautiful stones and appointments, looking up and around, slack-jawed, and Jesus's words that day must have sounded like a loud fart at a funeral. "You see all this stuff?" he asked, looking at the gold leaf and fabulous furnishings and ornate appointments and impressive wealth. "The days are coming, my friends, when all this that grabs your eye will be dust in the wind. Do not be fooled. Do not be led astray. The days are coming when someone will emerge saying they will be your Savior. Do not listen to them."

Jesus is not one to be distracted by all that glitters and gleams. He will be publicly executed a few days after saying these things. And I suspect these words contributed mightily to the building ire against him. Jesus was taking a much longer view into the future than most of us dare to take.

"But hey," he continues. "Fear not. You will indeed be hated, and some of you will even be put to death. But do not worry. Not a hair of your head will perish. I have got something for you that absolutely trumps all this upheaval. I will give you words and a wisdom that nobody can contradict." And it is here that I wish I could peer into the hearts and minds of those disciples. I wonder if they were thinking something like, "Say *what*, Old Bean? You'll give us *words* for all that is facing us? *Just words?* Well, thanks. Thanks a lot."

* * *

I have told you before that I have a fair number of friends outside the church who are either agnostic or atheist or somewhere in-between. They're among my very best friends, and I am grateful to God for them because they've pushed me (and not gently some-times) to ponder why in the world I continue to believe in God and place Jesus and his teachings first. Or at least try to place him first.

When I was a little kid, our family lived pretty close in Chatta-nooga to the Little Debbie factory. It was just a couple miles away in Collegedale, Tennessee. I ran around in our yard a lot, daydreaming about Daniel Boone. ("Daniel Boone was a man—yes, a *biiiggg* man!") Sorry about that. And Sky King and Johnny Quest and Bat Masterson. But I also had this idea that if the Little Debbie factory *blew up*, then a cloud of Swiss cake rolls would rain down on my street, and I'd be a happy little boy.

I told this story to one of my agnostic friends once, and he said, "Yeah, that is a funny story all right, Frank. Just about as funny as some of those Bible stories you are building your life around, buddy. Jesus is just about as likely to heal this world as God will rain down Oatmeal Creme Pies into your life. Wake up," he said. "These stories in your Bible are not real. The words of the one you call Lord are ludicrous in the land where we happen to live these days."

The disciples are in the temple. Jesus predicts a rather unnerving future. And then he says, "Hey, do not worry. *I will give you words*."

Now think about this with me, please. Is it any wonder his disciples took flight and abandoned this man a few days later? Maybe they started to abandon Jesus that very day in the temple. "I will give you words." Can't you almost hear what they're thinking, given the violent and unforgiving world in which they lived? *Yeah, right, Jesus*.

* * *

There is a line at the end of this temple tour today that really gives me pause as a pastor. Jesus uses the word "endurance" to describe the life of following him as a disciple. *Endurance.* We're in this discipleship stuff for the long haul, he seems to be saying. It will be like an endurance test. "By your endurance you will gain your souls."

A question: if we "gain our souls" through enduring with Jesus, is it also possible to lose them along the way?

* * *

As we near the end of another church year, Jesus shares some rather ominous predictions about life as we know it. But fear not, he says. *I will give you words.*

But we already have his words, do we not? He's given them to us already as a priceless gift. Words like: Share your wealth. Practice forgiveness and kindness. Live sacrificially in the shape of a cross. Pray for your enemies. Befriend the annoying.

His words, in many ways, are like life preservers floating in a sea of noise and distraction. However you voted, it is worth asking: Have we stopped listening to his words in favor of other voices?

Someone once said that overtly political sermons only reveal which periodicals the pastor reads at the parsonage. With that as a warning, it is still unwise (and unbiblical) to always avoid politics in the pulpit, especially during a presidential election where candidates make inflated promises that seem at times to border on the messianic. An eager electorate, sensing needed change, may unconsciously assign to candidates attributes and hopes that flirt with idolatry and misplaced faith.

Part of this sermon's purpose from November of 2016 was to name the simmering truth that could be palpably felt that morning all around the room: we are a divided nation, a divided community, and, therefore, a divided congregation in the wake of an election season that was perhaps unprecedented in its intense exchange of excessive heat and diminished light. My central theme statement for the sermon in this contentious context: "The words given to the disciples by Jesus usurp all other words."

At first glance, there's nothing earthshaking in this statement. But the theme was entirely pastoral (and even confrontational) on the first Sunday after the Tuesday vote. This was a sermon where shared confessional conviction in a common Apostles' Creed (spoken together soon after the sermon) was named aloud as a guiding allegiance that eclipses all other allegiances, including those of flag and country. A preacher often knows right away if a sermon has made an impact. With this one, the proverbial pin-drop could have been heard. I intentionally left longer than normal silences at the breaks in the sermon (indicated with three asterisks) to allow parishioners time to ponder and do their own reflecting.

Recall Luke 2:19, where Mary, just after giving birth to Jesus, "ponders [all these words] in her heart" that are newly knocking around internally. The Greek verb in this phrase is *symballo*—*sym* ("together") plus *ballo* ("to throw"). Sermons often need built-in periods of silent pondering, especially when a preacher "throws together" disparate ideas that are often kept separate (such as the oft-misunderstood separation of church and state) in the lives of many parishioners for a host of cultural reasons. Authentic conversion suggests that Jesus's teachings newly conceived in any of his disciples will need time to gestate before bearing mature fruit. A sermon needs proper pacing in this regard.

One (unexpected) result of this sermon was that people who had been at odds through a long and straining political season talked to one another on the way out of worship. No "Kum-Ba-Ya" moments occurred, to be sure, but I came away convinced of the Spirit's reconciling presence in worship that morning and the potential to heal a great divide. Authentic Christian community—whose identity and purpose can be formed and recalled through preaching—is one of the few remaining places where people of vastly different perspectives can come together in hopefully civil exchange and dare to call each other "brothers and sisters."

Craig Barnes describes a divisive issue at Princeton Seminary (that even spread beyond the seminary) involving an outside speaker who came to campus, and the power of local community to help heal the division as face-to-face opportunities for conversation were offered to those with differing perspectives. This was especially important for those who felt they didn't belong in the community:

> People who disagreed spoke with each other. This accountability to a community is what's missing in social media, and why the fire that jumped the road around campus continued to burn after the seminary itself had found its way forward. . . . I lost count of how many times I carefully explained that our community is centered in Christ. We all belong to him. If we are clear about that, we do not have to worry about the boundaries because the center will always hold.[11]

A sermon's theme statement should be short: a dozen words or less and, again, the product of a meaningful encounter with the selected Bible text in a variety of contexts earlier in the week leading up to Thursday.

Integrate All Facets of Ministry in the Preaching Process

By now, I hope it's apparent that a daily process of preaching leading up to the naming of a theme statement involves all the primary pastoral skills any congregation needs on a journey toward missional health. Pastors feel a great siren tug to be pulled hither and yon in the direction of a variety of important needs and issues. Sometimes this pull masks itself creatively in justifying one's pastoral "worth" to others via the church's business and busy-ness. "You're so busy, pastor!" Sometimes that wasn't even all that true, but I still enjoyed hearing it, which is rather warped if you think about it.

Congregational life can indeed move along at a dizzyingly frantic pace, with many committees, events, projects, and agendas vying for a pastor's time. This is especially true in the first year of a new call. Even though Lutherans have a historically helpful and well-defined job description for clergy to the "ministry of word and sacrament" (generally known by the leaders of congregations I have served), it is still incumbent upon the pastor to help shape a corporate understanding of what his or her primary role in congregational life is and is not.

Adopting various sermon habits soon out of seminary can be helpful in building a healthy pastoral identity and educating a congregation concerning the pastor's *raison d'etre*.[12] There will be many well-intentioned people in any parish who think they know exactly why a pastor is present on-site. An older man once told me that God had appointed him to be my personal "coach" in discovering how to be a pastor in that congregation. This was after twenty-five years of pastoral ministry in three different churches. I told him that the elected

84

congregation council would instead function nicely in such a role.

This is another reason why using pirated sermons from an Internet subscription service just isn't a good idea. Such sermons serve to subtly convince a new preacher that preaching is just another ministerial task to be checked off in a list of other pressing tasks. The truth is that a faithful preaching process shapes the entirety of one's ministry for the long haul. The spiritual habits we develop throughout the week in preparing for a Sunday sermon ground us in the very disciplines that have nourished pastors in their callings for centuries.

Don't settle for homiletical shortcuts. "Enter through the narrow gate; for the gate is wide and the road is easy that leads to destruction, and there are many that take it. For the gate is narrow and the road is hard that leads to life" (Matt. 7:13–14). Jesus offers this advice in proximity to the ominous words "I never knew you" (7:23), less a threat than a simple statement of truth.

Pastors are present in a congregation to help others know Jesus. Preaching can be difficult and exhausting work; it's never easy. But the various components of a faithful preaching process, all disciplines that strengthen a pastor's relationship with Christ, will be noticed and imitated over time by those seeking to be faithful disciples. "Brothers and sisters," wrote that brash first-century pastor, "join in imitating me, and observe those who live according to the example you have in us" (Phil. 3:17). Saint Paul wasn't bragging or engaging in theological grandstanding. He knew discipleship required guidance and apprenticing.

The prayer, textual wrestling, faithful conversation, study, openness to unexpected spiritual insight, portable on-the-go exegesis, traffic-light inspiration, shared agony amid suffering, and meetings infused with this Sunday's Scripture lessons—all part of a faithful preaching process—are the very disciplines a congregation of any era needs as they together strive for faithfulness to Jesus's Great Commission. "Go therefore and make disciples of all nations, baptizing them in the name of the Father and of the Son and of the Holy Spirit, and teaching them to obey everything that I have commanded you" (Matt. 28:19–20a).

Everything?

Tertullian was right. Disciples are made, not born.

The weekly disciplines inherent in a faithful process of preaching shape pastoral leadership in developing the ongoing growth of new and old disciples.

5

REFLECTING

A Pastor Looks Back

The following story ("Twenty-Fifth") is fictional. I wrote it (along with several other fictional tales with various pastors as the central characters) in the first year of my retirement, as I looked back upon a thirty-one-year career as a Lutheran minister. The stories helped me reflect upon the joys of the pastoral vocation, but also the emotional challenges inherent in three decades of funerals and often-agonizing incidents. I offer the story here as an honest interlude in the larger process of writing sermons just out of seminary. I'll offer a bit more commentary at the end of the story, specifically exploring how stories like this one shape a pastoral preaching imagination.

Twenty-Fifth

Another Sunday afternoon. He walks alone to his car, the only automobile left in the large parking lot. His flock filed out for the feast downtown at the local steak house about half an hour ago. When souls are filled, the stomach is never far behind. He's been at this long enough to know the order of human urges.

Tom always sits in the nave for a few minutes after his parishioners have departed. He prays a while, listening for the various voices who just shared concerns for coming surgeries, or worries about certain family members and friends. The pastoral receiving line after the service concludes is often a lot to take in all at once. He makes a few notes on the back of the worship bulletin with one of the short pencils, almost always dull, located on the back of each pew in narrow cylindrical holes just to the left of the hymnal racks.

The ancient oak pews creak slightly, shifting in release of carried weight. The tin roof pops as the high sun continues to expand sheets of metal, sounds all but inaudible during the loud return of the organ and the raised voices of gathered Lutherans offering praise to their creator and savior.

He reads the tenures of former pastors who've served Trinity Church, etched in stained glass on either side of the wide sanctuary, with years of service listed below each name. Tom has seen their pictures in congregational history books — serious eyes, long beards; clerics who ruled in stern authority and confident surety. At least they seem to exude such an air. He is one of twenty-four pastors who've served here since shortly before the Civil War. In his prayers following worship, he tries to imagine them standing in the pulpit up front and what they might have said at various times in South Carolina state history or during a particular challenge facing the nation.

Tom enjoys the solitary moments in the empty building when all the chatty voices have departed. He sits in the near-silence until Mary might worry why he's late for lunch. Noting the attendance for the morning, recorded by a team of ushers, he grabs a tattered briefcase from his church study, locks the front door, and heads out into the sunshine of a rare Sunday afternoon with no other meetings or visits.

A block away, a jogger waves — David, a doctor he has be-friended in town, a man who gave up God many years ago "along with the Tooth Fairy." Tom sometimes envies his friend's freedom.

Birds pass overhead, and a single raven perches atop the weathervane on the old clock tower. He wonders if the ancient bird knows his secrets, or whether it benefits anyone to bother keeping them anymore.

Each Sunday is the same. He mounts the high pulpit to speak. People full of hope or sadness or joy or sometimes anger lean into his words like small birds receiving seed from a backyard feeder. The occasional parishioner sleeps, but most listen attentively. He will give them that.

Pastor Tom stops to wave at his doctor friend, who points up to the church steeple without breaking stride. Tom looks up at the raven who calls out to other birds. Unlocking the car door and getting into the driver's seat, the minister is unsure whether he's even listening to his own words anymore.

* * *

"Thomas, care for God's people, bear their burdens, and do not betray their confidence. So discipline yourself in life and teaching that you preserve the truth, giving no occasion for false security or illusory hope. Be of good courage, for God has called you."

"Yes," he had vowed to his bishop. "And I ask God to help and guide me." Tom would need all three — courage, guidance, and help. He had no idea on that September day, at age twenty-eight, what he was really getting into.

He remembers cake and a reception and lots of well-wishers, including his parents and in-laws. He recalls the birth of their first child only two weeks earlier during a month that included moving into a parsonage in the Shenandoah Valley, erecting the crib, and unpacking their belongings.

The conference dean, announcing the ordination before the worship assembly at the conclusion of the liturgy, mistakenly inverted his middle and last names. "I present to you Pastor Michael Wilson Thomas!"

Tom's clergy colleagues still jokingly say the name snafu means the ordination was never really official.

* * *

David Martin is widely regarded in upstate South Carolina as an excellent orthopedic surgeon. Tom would be able to testify to this truth even if David hadn't perfectly executed his hip replacement, surgery he hardly notices two years later. The doctor listens well and asks good questions. Without coming across as opinionated, he expresses strong and well-considered convictions. The man reads more widely than any physician Tom has ever known.

"I decided to leave the church," David said over a cup of iced mocha at Main Street Coffee one morning, "when a priest told me our first child couldn't be baptized unless I believed in Jesus's bodily resurrection. I told the guy I loved Jesus and tried to live by his teachings, but just couldn't buy into a dead man walking around three days after an execution. It is a reasonable doubt, right, for a med-school graduate who was on a first-name basis with his human anatomy cadaver?"

Tom laughed and said David would fit right in with half his parishioners who confessed that part of the Apostles' Creed with their fingers crossed. "You should be grateful that all the afterlife bestsellers hadn't quite been published when your priest decided to interrogate you," said the pastor. "You know, the books about children dying, meeting their grandparents and miscarried siblings in heaven, and suddenly returning to life in a hospital room to describe all the celestial furniture they saw. You'd have had a field day with that stuff."

David shook his head and smiled, then turned serious. "Susan was a little upset when I spoke to a priest like that. And more upset when we decided to leave. She was raised Catholic. Her grandmother in New Jersey even kept a crucifix above the toilet in the bathroom. I'm sure that heaped a ton of guilt on Susan's poor brother when they visited their grandparents as teenagers and he wanted a private moment with the latest women's underwear catalog from Sears."

Tom could tell David things he had never found courage to share with a parishioner. In seminary, there was a recurring and rather dumb debate about whether a pastor should have close friends in the congregation. Tom understood all the red flags of such friendships, but knew parish life could be a pretty lonely existence without them. Mary and Tom had good friends at Trinity Church, but none as close as David and Susan.

It was nice to have a friend with whom Tom could share anything. David understood the importance and sanctity of confidentiality. It was also liberating to have someone listen to a pastor's own theological doubts without even a hint of condescension or judgment.

Additionally, the skeptical orthopedist had another gift. He could mix a Friday afternoon gin and tonic better than anyone Tom had ever known.

* * *

Early in Pastor Wilson's ministry in the Shenandoah Valley, an unexpected death really shook him, and also scared Mary.

It occurred shortly after they'd been summoned to the home of one of the congregation's aging matriarchs, Peggy Snopes, who was almost blind and lived in the heart of apple country in the valley near the low ridge of North Mountain. The pastor, his young wife, and their new baby, Hannah, sat in the morning sunshine of Peggy's high-ceilinged parlor. She served apple dumplings and coffee. There were assigned seats.

"And you," said Peggy, pointing a long and crooked finger at Tom, "shall be called *Pastor Wilson*. I will have none of this infernal modern practice of referring to an ordained man of God by his first name." Tom nodded an assent and said that was just fine; she could call him anything she wanted. She glared at her new pastor for a few seconds.

Peggy then turned to Mary. "And you, my dear." The same finger found its mark. "You shall be referred to as *Mrs. Wilson*. Informality is also the devil's handiwork when it comes to disregarding the high calling of a pastor's wife." Mary fought back a laugh and was thankful that baby Hannah provided a handy distraction.

Tom spoke to divert attention away from Mary. "That's fine. We certainly don't want to offend anyone. But it's only fair to ask, What shall we call you?"

"Oh," said the old woman, whose glasses, thick as Coke bottles, gave her eyes an owlish appearance. "You can call me Peggy."

Everyone in the room laughed at that. So hard, in fact, that baby Hannah woke up and started to cry.

A month later, on a Monday afternoon, Tom heard from their pediatrician, Dr. Daniel Malone. Tom thought it was sort of odd to receive a call directly from the doctor rather than a member of the office staff. He and Mary had just been to the doctor three days prior for Hannah's well-baby check.

"Pastor, you need to come right away. Eric Dellinger's not breathing. His parents asked me to call you." Eric was a three-year-old in the congregation who had been born with a variety of respiratory challenges.

"Yes, we're all here," said the doctor. "Come in the side door. One of my nurses will be looking for you. They'll take you back. Please come as quickly as you can."

When he returned home to the parsonage later that afternoon, Tom told Mary he had never seen such anguish on anyone's face. Little Eric was on an examining table in a room across from the nurses' station. Melvin and Katie Dellinger were holding each other, leaning across the table and touching their son. Katie sometimes sobbed quietly, resting her head softly on Eric's little chest, occasionally releasing a haunting, keening wail. The lingering echo would later awaken Tom in his sleep.

The child's mouth had turned slightly blue by the time of Tom's arrival. Otherwise, Eric looked like a normal little boy, perfectly formed. He appeared to be smiling.

Without speaking or asking questions about Eric, Mary held Tom in the doorway of the parsonage nursery late that afternoon. They both looked in at their sleeping baby.

"I tried to pray," Tom told her. "I tried, but nothing would come. I didn't know what to say. Here they needed a pastor who might offer some sort of word for a senseless moment, and I couldn't help at all. I think we mumbled the Lord's Prayer together. I hugged them. I made the sign of the cross on Eric's forehead. At least I did that much. But I wasn't prepared for what I saw this afternoon. I'm not sure I can do this."

Peggy Snopes hugged him at the church door the following Sunday. She said, "That was perhaps the most powerful funeral sermon I have ever heard, Pastor Wilson. And beginning today, I am calling you Tom."

It felt good to be enveloped by the love and care that flowed from that congregation in the days and weeks that followed. But mostly the young pastor couldn't shake a nagging thought—how much he had in common with the disciple who had all the doubts. Even their names were the same.

* * *

"You know, today happens to be the twenty-fifth anniversary of my ordination."

It was a Friday afternoon after work. Tom and David were sitting in Adirondack chairs on the doctor's backyard deck, sipping gin and tonics in late September in the South Carolina sun. A slight hint of autumn was in the air. One sweetgum and two dogwood trees were beginning to show color.

"Well, here's to you, Rev. I see quite a bit of pain in my work. But I suspect you've seen a lot more suffering. I don't know how you do it. I manipulate bones and patch people up. Sometimes they get better; other times, age or simple non-compliance affects their recovery. But I never have to plant people in the ground."

"And I never have to use a knife on people," Tom said. "Although there have been a few times I've wanted to wield a sharpened blade on certain parishioners. I've thought about carrying a Sunday shiv under my robe to surprise the unsuspecting whose heads are bowed with eyes closed at the communion table. You'd come to see me in jail, wouldn't you, Doc?"

David tinkled the cubes of ice in his glass and took another sip of gin. "All kidding aside, after a quarter-century of work as a pastor in two different states in a variety of settings, what's been the toughest part of your job?"

Tom let the question hang in the air. He pointed silently to a hawk that flew low across the back of David's yard, perching on the branch of an oak tree at the far corner of the property.

"Like you," Tom said, "I think most people have questions about their faith. I've decided that one of the purposes of the sermon is to give voice to mysteries in this life that we all feel in our hearts but aren't quite ready to state out loud to each other. I'm not sure where that comes from, the hesitancy to question publicly. The Bible is full of faithful people who bring very difficult questions to God."

A half-minute of silence passed before David answered. "You know that I've given up on church, but I do sneak in occasionally to hear you, and slip out before the last hymn. I'm familiar with your style. You're an effective preacher. You like raising questions. That's part of your theological *modus operandi.* I suspect you take a certain glee in raising controversial topics. But that isn't what I asked. What's been the hardest part?"

* * *

With a young father-to-be, Tom walks the long corridors of a community hospital. A nurse answers the occasional voice calling for help from within a darkened room. The rhythmic beep of an empty IV-bag chirps in tandem to her steps and then fades away. Otherwise, the hospital is eerily quiet this night, in contrast to the bustle and mayhem of late afternoon.

Chris and Jan have been told the news. Their new baby, a little girl, will be born dead a few hours from now after induced labor. The word "scan" seems to always reveal so much more than a glance to some implied horizon. The umbilical cord had wrapped tightly around the baby's neck. With months of happy movements, now there were none.

It's three a.m. The pastor and the young father walk in silence for what seems like miles, switching floors, occasionally popping outside to walk the paved loop around the hospital boundary.

From the track, the two men watch a car park at the glass doors of the emergency room and discharge a limping passenger with a wound or some unknown ailment. Otherwise, it's dark and still. They could be walking under the stars in the pastor's neighborhood in a small town in southwest Virginia, site of Tom's second parish.

The labor attending the arrival of a healthy child is hard enough. The sadness and anguish coloring this delivery seem unspeakably coupled with the contractions, especially within the context of the small hospital's maternity ward, where all parents except two are filled with gratitude and joy. There is no other room for the stillbirth to occur. The contrast between gladness and pain seems inexpressibly cruel.

The two men haven't spoken for at least half an hour, and then the oldest of questions. "Pastor Tom, why would a good God allow this to happen?"

Sometimes angry parishioners want answers to their questions. They want explanations, even divine accountability. They seek experienced testimony from someone familiar with suffering.

Tom senses this is not one of those moments. Chris isn't interested in words. He just wants permission to ask.

"I don't know," says the pastor. "I don't know why. But God is here and walks with us."

They walk another lap and return to Jan's room. They pray. The labor pains have intensified.

* * *

It was Tom's turn to tinkle the ice cubes. "There was this time in Virginia, our second town; a young couple whose child was stillborn. I walked with that dad most of the night. We didn't say much."

David angled his Adirondack even closer toward his friend. Tom continued his long stare out toward the trees where the hawk remained perched.

"The dead baby looked almost perfect. I was glad the nurse asked Jan, the mother, if she wanted to hold the little girl. I've heard that sometimes stillborn children are taken away pretty quickly from the parents. These two held her for some time — little Savannah. The nurse even took a picture for Jan and Chris. She moved through that sad room with very few words, but her actions spoke so much. That nurse was a godsend."

"I'm sure you were, too," said David.

"I prayed. I don't remember the words. We all sat on the hospital bed and cried. I don't remember much of the drive home that morning. The sun was coming up. Mary met me at the door. I collapsed into her arms and just couldn't stop crying. I think Hannah, our oldest, up for school, peeked into our bedroom and saw me sobbing, absolutely wracked with grief and tears — my whole body bunched and shaking in a sad clump. It scared me."

"You were scared for her to see you that way?"

"In a way, yes. But I was mostly afraid I was losing my faith."

On the deck, Tom's eyes were filled with tears. The sun was setting. David rose and said, "I want to show you something."

* * *

Tom knew about a caregiver's shopworn need for "personal bound-aries." His bishop spoke of erecting professional boundaries each time he talked to a group of pastors, but Tom often felt the guy was mostly trying to protect the church from the recent spate of clergy sexual misconduct lawsuits.

Driving to the cemetery behind the hearse in his aging Toyota Corolla, Tom wondered what sort of "boundary" the bishop might suggest for his ministry with Jan and Chris.

The service back at the church had been packed—a lot of young people, friends of the young couple. Tom guessed that most of the attendees hadn't been to a church service in many years. He chose an old text from Isaiah, a promise close to three millennia old. "For I am about to create new heavens and a new earth; the former things will not be remembered or come to mind. No more shall there be an infant that lives but a few days, or an old person who does not live out a lifetime."

"This may not be a broken promise," Tom said in his short sermon based upon Isaiah's ancient words. "But today it sure feels like it." The family had requested communion for the service, a relative rarity for Lutherans at a funeral. Tom noticed many of those who reached for the bread and wine looked him squarely in the eye and slowly nodded their heads as if in agreement with his words.

Many worshipers remained at the graveside with Jan and Chris, even as the mortuary workers began to shovel dirt on the undersized coffin from the small mound of earth beside the fam-ily plot. Several family members added their own handfuls. Young cousins each dropped a single rose into the grave. Tom stood off to the side until the last mourners started to head back to their cars.

One man, Chris's uncle, turned and headed back toward the pastor. The uncle thanked Tom. They spoke awhile beside the child's grave. Before walking away, the uncle repeated the same line that had opened the conversation: "I don't know how you do what you do."

During the drive back to town, Tom remembered the anguished scene at the hospital. He recalled baby Savannah in her parents' arms. He saw his own daughter's face in the door of the bedroom, wondering why her daddy was in such pain.

He heard again the uncle's words at the graveside.

"I'm not sure I know, either," Tom said.

* * *

As Tom and David left the back-porch deck and walked across the backyard toward the woods, the pastor on his ordination anniversary remembered his friends in seminary who had decided against becoming ministers, at least in the traditional sense. Their ministry had led them in different directions: to teaching, carpentry, plumbing, the national park service.

For some reason, Tom always felt more connected to classmates who were uncertain about their call. It was one reason he had come to love David. His honesty about God seemed far more sincere than the confident pomposity Tom heard spewed at most clergy gatherings.

David spoke slowly as he walked. "You know, Susan and the kids have started back to church. I'm grateful they've found a home with the Lutherans. You can look for me on occasion, of course, but I'm certainly blessed to have an understanding wife who puts up with my Sunday jogs while she loads the family passel into the van for church school. Am I right?"

Tom laughed. "Every time I've ever mentioned anything about doing something else, Mary reminds me that any vocational change will unequivocally mean my butt will still warm some church's Sunday pew. Yes, you are blessed."

"We're just about there," David said. "Just through this last row of trees."

On a bank above a small creek that bordered the property, three rows of stuffed animals sat on small logs in a circle of light shining through the forest canopy. Tom noted a dog, a duck, an ostrich, and a beaver among the animals. They sat upright, with paws, hands, and flippers folded in their laps, facing a small table covered with a cloth. A ceramic plate and metal cup, resembling a chalice, rested on the table. Behind the table was a doll dressed in a white robe with her arms raised in blessing. A green band of material was draped over the doll's shoulders.

David looked at Tom. The pastor was crying for the second time that day. "So, what happens when it rains?"

"She runs out here and gathers them all together under that tarp. We had a thunderstorm the other night, and she woke me up. I had to come out here with a flashlight."

"It is Judith, right?" asked Tom.

"Yep, she says she wants to be a pastor. She wants to be like you. Go figure."

*   *   *

Another Sunday. Congregants have filed out through the pastoral receiving line and are now downtown at lunch. Details swim through the pastor's head. The church is quiet except for the creaks of empty pews and an occasional ping from the warm roof.

A lot can happen in a pastor's life over several decades. Perhaps it's best that some of it is difficult to recall and may even remain forgotten. Maybe giving them a short memory is how God dupes ministers into accepting such a job.

Tom shakes his head at the notion and laughs softly, aloud. It has been a good life, an honorable vocation. He still finds it amazing that people trust him with so much of their lives. Perhaps they've seen in him an invitation to question and examine their own faith. He hopes so.

Tom straightens the hymnals on the row he's chosen for his weekly time of silence after the service. He lifts a pencil stub from its worn resting place and makes a few notes on a folded bulletin.

He prays awhile, then rises and walks out into the empty parking lot, looking east toward town for his friend.

Give Voice to Mystery

At one point in "Twenty-Fifth," Pastor Tom reflects upon one of the purposes of the sermon: "to give voice to mysteries in this life that we all feel in our hearts but aren't quite ready to state out loud to each other."

The Bible is full of agonizing questions. And so are the hearts and minds of most parishioners who take faith seriously. But the expanse between having questions and daring to state them out loud is often rather wide and daunting. "I didn't know we could ask such questions in church" is a statement I've heard numerous times. Sermons can serve as a public invitation for a community to candidly admit that even though they confess a common creed each Sunday in a single voice, that doesn't mean an absence of questions always accompanies the corporate recitation of the ancient words.

When pastors are regularly vulnerable and candid about their own faith questions that surface in ancient lectionary texts, a climate of common searching and discovery can slowly take shape in the congregation in cyclical observance of the church year. If a community is serious about authentic discipleship in the name of Jesus, the community will together experience agonizing and befuddling incidents (such as the faith-shaking funerals of the two dead children in the story, incidents from my own ministry) that are not easily explained or forgotten. "We want to love God with the heart," writes Tom Long, "but we also want to love God with our mind, too. We want to do more than lament and shout and raise the fist; we also want to understand."[1]

Offering easy answers when faced with suffering ultimately helps no one. In one congregation[2] I served, one of our stated "desired outcomes" specifically addressed such concerns: "We will develop a local, on-the-street reputation where a diversity of people—unbaptized adults, people who question, skeptics, and religious seekers—might come to explore Christianity." Sermons can help form such a community by daring to be honest about the agonies already present in our hearts that search for meaning and voice.

I have always appreciated an old scene from the book of Daniel, easy to miss among a den of lions, a fiery furnace, and strange handwriting on the wall. In chapter ten, Daniel (in exile) has been praying, fasting, and mourning for a full three weeks with no clear answer from God. He's persistent in prayer even when insight is elusive. Finally, Daniel receives a visit from a divine messenger. "Do not fear, Daniel, for from the first day that you set your mind to gain understanding and to humble yourself before your God, your words have been heard, and I have come because of your words" (10:12). The messenger and his partner, the angel Michael, had been delayed in a conflict with "the prince of the kingdom of Persia" (10:13). They were tag-teaming the evil prince, so to speak, until one could break away and aid could reach Daniel "to help you understand what is to happen to your people at the end of days" (10:14).

This delightfully odd story acknowledges both the Nicene Creed's claim of mysteries "seen and unseen" and the common lag time between faithful prayer and delayed insight. A sermon can faithfully bring to articulation the agonies and questions inherent during the in-between waiting period— sometimes weeks, years, or even a lifetime.

In the short story, I tried to portray Pastor Tom as a human being who also has faith struggles like anyone else who strives to believe in God's promises. As a parish pastor discovers a percolated and marinated theme emerging from the texts appointed for the coming Sunday, it is at least occasionally appropriate for one who dares to stand and speak from the community's pulpit to be utterly honest about his or her own struggles with faith. Like Daniel, a preacher uses the vagaries of the pastoral calling "to gain understanding and to humble yourself before your God."

God listens. Insight often takes a long time. Pastors dare to believe that divine help can come "because of our words."

6
FRIDAY

Writing

Trust the Stone-Breaking Word

With several friends, I recently hiked up nearby Table Rock (3,124 feet), one of the highest peaks in upstate South Carolina. It was a beautiful day—three-and-a-half miles up; waves of geologic time.

We walked down the smooth rock face and found a cleft where a small tree grew—impossibly, it seemed. Two steps forward and 1,500 feet down. Across the gorge, Raven Cliff Falls dropped vertically, hundreds of gallons per second, carving an impressive notch in a ridge known as Caesars Head.

Paleontologist Stephen Jay Gould (1941–2002) compares the length of recorded human history to what was once called "the king's yard"—the distance between the royal shoulder and the tip of his middle finger. Symbolically, the span represents all of geologic time. Gould suggests that if one were to take a small file and make a single pass across the king's middle fingernail, the minute droppings that reach the floor would depict human longevity on earth.

Now factor in space. Based on the discoveries of the Hubble telescope, scientists now believe there are *nine galaxies* for every person on the planet. Assuming just over seven billion souls, that's a lot of galaxies—a perspective that boggles the mind, especially when recalling that our solar system fits into just one.

I sat on Table Rock thinking what an incredible gift it is to breathe and see and love—the years stretching backward and forward, all the innumerable hours. How God takes notice of us. How our decisions and words truly matter. And I thought of the first seven verses of the forty-third chapter of Isaiah, describing God's relentless love for humanity. "I have called you by name, you are mine" (43:1). Equipped with this divine love, God's people can presumably pass through rivers and even walk through fire (43:2).

I take this to mean that nothing can really "get" us—cancer, terrorism, death itself—because God's already got us. "You are precious in my sight" (43:4). If this is true, is there really *anything* to fear, including all the challenges inherent in a first call out of seminary that in some locales seem insurmountable?

These verses are even more striking considering the eight that precede these seven in the book of Isaiah. There God is white-hot with anger, incensed with the wayward behavior of his people. "Who is blind but my servant?" asks God. "All of them are trapped in holes and hidden in prisons" (42:19, 22). It is an overwhelming declaration of guilt and an interesting perspective for a new pastor called to a congregation perhaps struggling with past mistakes and fresh guilt.

The end of chapter 42 offers no hint of what's coming in 43. The verdict is read. *But the sentencing never arrives.*

Instead: "I have called you by name (and, in spite of your mistakes), you are mine."

Jesus stood there in the water that day and heard a voice. "You are my Son, the beloved; with you I am well pleased" (Luke 3:22). The voice in the river echoed that of Isaiah, who, about six hundred years before, addressed people in exile, people who were enslaved by their own mistakes and heard something wildly unexpected: *I have called you by name, you are mine.*

Is it possible that this watery declaration, this confident baptismal proclamation of his identity, gave Jesus the courage to live the way he did? To befriend the guilty? To declare mercy to those who did not deserve such? To embody in his own life the promises of a God who loves recklessly?

I like to think so. Jesus's ministry in the Synoptic Gospels gets underway only after these unconditionally accepting words. If that's true for Jesus, isn't it also true of the man's followers? And ministry-shaping for those called to lead his followers? That the words we hear at baptism set us apart to be agents of mercy with people who may well deserve another verdict?

I sometimes think of my favorite Wendell Berry poem before sitting down to write a sermon. "Creation Myth" describes two brothers in the Appalachian hills on a warm summer's night. Bill awakens and walks onto the cabin porch to cool off. He hears his brother, McKinley, arriving home late, heading through the dark woods and then down through the open pasture. Bill knows where his brother is in the farm's topography, but McKinley is disoriented. Amused, Bill allows his brother to wander in the darkness until McKinley "approached something really to fear," the nearby quarry pool.

Bill then loudly calls out his brother's name from the porch into the darkness, orienting his steps in the field, placing "the map of it in his head."[1]

Across the canyon of that wilderness, water flowed down from Caesars Head. Water flows down today and tomorrow and many tomorrows hence—toppling old and new Caesars and any sham power that stands in the way of God's gospel proclamation. The water of God directs a preacher's gospel orientation when we get lost. "There is a river whose streams make glad the city of God, the holy habitation of the Most High" (Ps. 46:4). Our proclamation efforts join innumerable tributaries over the centuries as the church streams toward God's long-planned reign.

The church is comprised of citizens of a new realm, even when we forget this and become disoriented, even when we fail to embody the grace that formed us. *I have called you by name, you are mine.* The words provide a map ahead.

Words spoken by a God who could make a compelling case against any of us. Words that break apart stone, reorient the lost, and create a whole new world.

Write Your Sermon: Four Observations

Regardless of eventual predilection in sermon delivery style—complete manuscript, outline, or extemporaneity—it's important for new pastors to strongly consider writing sermons in full on a particular day of the week. I wrote sermons on Friday mornings for thirty-one years. This doesn't mean the occasional emergency never interrupted that time, but carving out a weekly four-hour period for uninterrupted writing, away from the church building, paid immense dividends in shaping the quality of my preaching over time. Sharing the existence of this Friday discipline with congregation leaders also served to protect and honor the time. Several parishioners offered prayer for their pastor during this Friday writing time—an unexpected gift.

I honestly know very few pastors who are able to preach effective sermons without any notes at all. I've heard a handful of powerful extemporaneous sermons. I've also heard many rambling and poorly focused proclamation efforts that left me wondering if the preacher had spent much time thinking about the Bible text before deciding to open his or her mouth. (Forgive me, Jesus.) Even seasoned pastors who are blessed with strong mnemonic gifts usually choose to write sermons and then commit them to memory. Tom Long captures well what's at stake in any chosen sermon delivery method:

> The careful advance selection of apt words, phrases, and images for sermons is an act of ministry and much to be preferred over the sloppy and haphazard use of language that can result when we search for wording on our feet. The thoughtful composition of our sermons, heedfully selecting the language best suited for this congregation's hearing, is a way of taking seriously our responsibility to the listeners. On the other hand, the cumbersome reading of a manuscript can strain the interaction between preacher and hearers to the vanishing point.[2]

In the next chapter I'll share more concerning the homiletical movement from writing toward delivery. For now, consider these four observations as one pastor's encouragement to spend time with pen or keyboard.

Writing will help clearly frame the entry point of your sermon's theme.

It has been said that a sermon's introduction should be attention-getting to awaken the interest of a distracted and wandering mind. I agree that the introduction should be tightly focused and engender curiosity about the sermon's future content, but a preacher already has the attention of the congregation after reading the gospel lesson and offering a prayer that might hint at the theme. The more accurate truth is that it's easy to *lose* the congregation's attention in the first minute of the sermon with throwaway lines such as "It's good to see everyone here on this beautiful morning" or "What marvelous weather on this Seventeenth Sunday after Pentecost." The purpose of a sermon is to bring the congregation into an encounter with God's word, listening for God's voice and direction at a particular juncture in liturgical time. Careful writing will help clear away any chatty and unintended clutter from this primary purpose and set a tone for discovery. Novelist Benjamin Percy writes:

> Anticipation satisfies us in a way acquisition does not. . . . It is the way we are wired. We need to have something to look forward to. Prizes are the shiniest before they're won, just as monsters are scariest before they're seen. That is why Melville kept his white whale hidden so long, a shadowy surge, a pale mass breaking the surface in the distance.

Jules Verne treated his sea-shrouded squid in the same way. This is the power of temporary blindness.[3]

Percy's thoughts here aren't exactly analogous to writing a sermon, but they're worth pondering. Sometimes sermons fail because the preacher telegraphs the form and direction of the sermon early on, offering instant clarity from the very beginning: "Today I want to talk about King David's adultery and three ways we might avoid his mistakes in our modern era." Perhaps such a tack might be occasionally useful, but a regular diet of telegraphed sermonic direction is a sure recipe for a wandering mind, almost an invitation to think about other things while waiting for the next point in the list. The discipline of writing will help immensely in crafting an introduction that is faithful to the biblical text but leaves the listener a bit unsettled and curious.

I offer the following introduction not as a model of the form, but as an example of how careful attention to entry points can set a certain tone. This introduction was offered in a university setting[4] late in the 2017 Pentecost season. The central preaching text was part of Paul's letter from prison to the church in Philippi, specifically: "I want to know Christ and the power of his resurrection and the sharing of his sufferings by becoming like him in his death" (3:10). This introduction was offered immediately following a short prayer after the lectionary readings:

I want a secure retirement. I want a Republican in the White House. I want my children to be happy. I want to make a million dollars. I want everything to stay the same at my church. I want a Democrat in the White House. I want our national economy to be fixed. I want to be loved and admired. I want our enemies to pay for what they've done. I want Clemson to beat South Carolina again this year. I want recognition and esteem. I want my way. *I want.*

It was interesting to note from the pulpit that morning the curiosity (and amusement) on the faces of certain parishioners as they heard the conflicting claims of the second and sixth desires. These opening sentences of the sermon served to introduce a thematic conflict: our waking "wants" may not jibe with what Christ (speaking through Saint Paul) desires for his church. Writing out a sermon will help tighten a sermon's introduction to the theme without giving away too much. This intriguing connection becomes exponentially more difficult to make when attempted orally without any written preparation at all, on the fly.

Writing will help restate the content of a Bible passage for a culture that is increasingly unfamiliar with scriptural scope.

Nearing one-fifth of the way through the twenty-first century, one of the most important functions of the sermon may be the creative retelling of a Bible text, especially a text with connections in a wider scriptural narrative. Even well-known stories may be unfamiliar to a new generation of listeners whose encounter with the Bible outside of Sundays is possibly minimal. Sitting in the same pew on any Sunday morning may be a man who's brand-new to Christianity, a single parent who's recently returned to worship after an absence of some length, and an older couple who've been members of the church since the early days of the congregation's origins. How does the sermon address such a variety of listeners?

I have always enjoyed David Sedaris's description of learning French in Paris while enrolled in a beginning language class. Attendees from all over the world comprised the class. One day the topic of conversation turned to Christianity, and a Moroccan woman had no idea what was meant by the word "Easter." Various class members tried to explain. Sedaris records the exchange:

> The Poles led the charge to the best of their ability. "It is," said one, "a party for the little boy of God who call his self Jesus. . . . He call his self Jesus and then he die one day on two morsels of lumber." The rest of the class jumped in, offering bits of information that would have given the pope an aneurysm. "He die one day and then he go above of my head to live with your father." . . . Nothing we said was of any help to the Moroccan student. . . . I wondered then if, without the language barrier, my classmates and I could have done a better job making sense of Christianity, an idea that sounds pretty far-fetched to begin with.[5]

Sedaris's whimsical reflection describing one attempt to transmit the faith might serve as a cautionary flag to preachers attempting to share the gospel with an increasingly diverse congregation of listeners. Not every listener is equally familiar with the story.

Here's a portion of a sermon I preached in October of 2013 based upon Jacob's famous wrestling match in the night (Gen. 32:22–32) prior to his reunion with Esau. They hadn't seen each other in twenty years.

"Loved and Limping"

Harry Emerson Fosdick, the great preacher from Riverside Church in New York City (in the middle third of the twentieth century), had an excellent word of caution for pastors like me. "Only the preacher," he once warned, "proceeds still upon the idea that folk come to church desperately anxious to discover what happened to the Jebusites."[6] I hear that, Dr. Fosdick. The devil, of course, is in the details. But when it comes to the Bible, I think *God* can be found there too.

So, look with me at the first six words of this old lesson from Genesis. "The same night Jacob got up." *The same night Jacob got up*. He got up and he packed together all his belongings, all his animals, his two wives, two maids, and eleven children. And this whole entourage crosses the Jabbok River. *In the middle of the night*. Now I don't know if you've ever crossed a river at night on foot. It is not for the faint of heart.

This is strange enough. But verse 21 of chapter 32 (not printed in your bulletin today) suggests that Jacob and family and aforesaid mooing, squawking menagerie had *already settled in* for the night around a cozy campfire before they crossed that river. The animals had calmed down. The children were presumably dreaming.

As you may recall, Jacob married two sisters (Leah and Rachel). I cannot imagine the marital dynamic of being a husband for two sisters at the same time, but they seem to be getting along as the sun sets and supper dishes are put away. All is quiet. Let's say the stars are out and everyone is making peaceful slumbering sounds around the camp. Everyone except Jacob. He pops out of his bedroll and says, "Okay, everybody, I know you're cozy there in your sleeping bags and all. Sorry for interrupting your sweet dreams, but we're packing up and moving. Yes, you heard that right. We're moving to a new campsite across the river, and I don't want to hear a single word of complaining."

And they all get up, pack their duffel bags, and cross the river in the middle of the night. Can you imagine doing this with eleven children? I frankly cannot. Once they get settled on the other side, Jacob then *crosses back* over the river (two nocturnal crossings for our hero), and he sleeps alone, apart from his family. To state the utterly obvious: Jacob is a restless, troubled man. He's worried about something and cannot sleep. Does that ever happen to you? What wakes you up in the middle of the night? What causes you to pace around sometimes after midnight? We have a whole pharmacological industry for sleep disorders. Problems often seem larger after bedtime, right? Even little things are magnified way out of proportion around three a.m.

Do you remember *why* Jacob could easily star in a commercial for Lunesta? Poor Jacob is about to have a reunion. Reunions are often fraught with anxiety, to be honest—high school reunions, family reunions. Many people avoid reunions like the plague. We often bring a lot of baggage and memories into such events. Like no other gathering, a reunion is where you simply cannot escape your past—past behaviors, past dorkiness, past mistakes. There's nothing like a reunion to resurrect and rub your face in the past. Reunions are bread and butter for most working therapists.

On this night with all the river crossings, Jacob is about to experience a reunion with his brother Esau. And if you know the story, you will recall that it didn't end well with Jacob and Esau the last time they were together. Jacob stole his brother's birthright and stole his brother's family blessing—with the deceitful help of his mother, by the way, who never hid the fact that she loved Jacob best. (This was a family that was fairly dysfunctional before we knew that word.) Esau was incensed about all this, absolutely livid over this behavior and he vowed to kill Jacob if he could ever get his hands around his brother's neck.

Well, it's been twenty years since Jacob fled and Esau made that vow. Now, word has gotten back to Jacob that Esau is heading his way, only a day's journey down the trail. A few verses before this story, Jacob prays a foxhole sort of prayer to God: "Deliver me please, O LORD, from the hand of my brother, for I am afraid of him—he may come and kill us all, the mothers with the children."[7] Maybe you can understand why this particular reunion is laden with anxiety for poor Jacob. Why he cannot get to sleep this particular night, crossing back and forth through a river with only the stars to guide him.

I offered this detailed background in the sermon to help shed light (the assigned lectionary pericope is only eleven verses long) on the one who then jumps out of the shadows and wrestles with Jacob until morning. Verse 24 reports that this is "a man," and verse 25 says "the man." But then verse 28 suggests that Jacob wrestled with "God *and* humans." And verse 30 finally reports that Jacob has "seen God face-to-face." Who exactly was in the ring with our hero? There is delightful ambiguity here concerning the identity of Jacob's wrestling partner. Tradition is divided in this regard. Some say it was an angel; some say it was God. Some suggest it was even Esau himself jumping into the fray. I like to think it was a combination of all three, tag-teaming; that's the way it is with anxiety in the night. What's going on with us *on earth* can never be fully separated and hidden away from God *in heaven*. We wrestle with the bed sheets, sweating with anxiety and fear, and realize that our earthly worries are also inherently theological in nature. "You have striven with God *and* humans, Jacob." Yes, that is usually the way of it. Not one or the other—both.

In the sermon I wanted to stress that God often can't just wiggle his nose and make everything better. God isn't the instant "fixer" we often want him to be. We must go *through* our past, however painful, rather than pretend it never happened.

That last sentence is often a central reason why people come to church in the first place—trying to make sense of things, seeking absolution and insight from events of the past; some of those events still haunt them in the night. Collectively, a congregation hauls a lot of emotional baggage into worship every Sunday, during the confession and again at the altar for communion.

Creatively retelling a centuries-old Bible story to help modern people find their place in the story can be a powerful function of the sermon. Few preachers are born storytellers, able to pull this off on the fly. Writing the story from a fresh perspective can be an issue of hospitality. The theme of your sermon will shape the perspective you choose for the retelling.

Notice how fiction writer Joseph Heller enters the mind of David after the Bathsheba incident and records the deteriorating relationship between God and the king:

> Until he lifted my sin from me and placed it on my baby, God and I were as friendly as anyone could imagine. I inquired for guidance whenever I wished to. He could always be counted upon to respond. Our talks were sociable and precise. No words were wasted. "Should I go down to Keilah and save the city?" I asked while still a fugitive in Judah. "Go down to Keilah and save the city," He answered help-

fully. "Should I go up into Hebron in Judah and allow the elders to crown me king?" I asked after receiving news of Saul's death and completing my famous elegy. "Why not?" God obliged me in reply.[8]

And how Brian Doyle describes the physical stature of Jesus while alluding to three different Bible stories in creative economy:

> But he must have been slender, even slight, for he was a tireless walker, and could fast for forty days at a time; and he must have been wiry strong too, for the one time he popped a gasket and lost his temper altogether he tossed tables and moneychangers around like Frisbees in the very temple where he had given his mother such nervy lip when he was twelve years old.[9]

Retelling a Bible story in writing is always an exercise in interpretation, never finished with any text in any century, employing many of the homiletical tools of tenor, tone, and context discussed earlier.

Writing the sermon develops employment of a controlling metaphor which will increase thematic consistency and aid in ease of listening.

This statement is especially true with funeral sermons. Worshipers at a funeral service sometimes bring along a host of competing emotions: sadness, doubt, exhaustion, guilt, and anger, to name a few. It's often tough for someone in the pew to focus on a funeral homily, sometimes because too many themes and too many Bible texts (I counted fourteen Scripture passages at one funeral service I attended a couple years ago) overload a listener's ability to comprehend.

"Grief," writes Richard Lischer, "is a series of caves—dark, multiple, and unfathomed. You do not explore them. You fall into them. Which means you are constantly righting yourself and daily, sometimes hourly, recovering from little plunges into unrequited longing and despair."[10] A controlling metaphor, revisited throughout the funeral homily, can be a great gift to worshipers. The obituary has already been written and printed. No need to revisit those details. What can the preacher uniquely say about the presence of Christ in this particular person, accompanying worshipers whose various "little plunges" have preceded their entrance into the worship space and now assemble once again around the room?

Ken was a beloved pharmacist for over forty years in our little town. He literally knew everyone—their health histories; their mommas and daddies, as we say in the South; their secrets. When Ken died after a long illness, the church was absolutely packed for the Sunday afternoon funeral. The sermon was based upon Ezekiel 47:1–9 and the water flowing out of the temple, slowly increasing in depth. Here is an excerpt:

I went online the other day, curious about the little town where Ken grew up. I tried to imagine him as a little boy riding around the streets of Yemassee, South Carolina, on his bicycle with that same easy laugh and impressive ears and eyes that almost disappeared when he grinned. Don't you think Ken must have been an interesting little boy whose curiosity took him all over the nooks and crannies of that little town, a third of the size of Walhalla?

I discovered a good bit about the Native American origins of the town, but had to search awhile to learn what the word "Yemassee" actually means. As far as I can tell, it means "gentle." Our friend grew up in a town whose name means "gentle." Talk about destiny. For little Ken surely grew up to be a gentle man. A gentleman, in the classic sense of that word.

Anyone who decides to be a public servant in a small community knows that one's time is largely no longer one's own. A pharmacist hangs out a shingle and welcomes an entire town into his life—their stories, their hopes, their joys, and their flaws. It's a job that requires the patience of Job. And we know that even Job lost it at times.

An irate customer standing at the counter can know nothing of the man in line just behind him, struggling with a silent illness. Nor can that same customer know of a woman in the store fifteen minutes ago who needed medicine but couldn't afford it and walked out with her prescription filled anyway with kindness and patience.

A pharmacist, like any public servant, knows more about the pulse of a town (its secrets) than most. And carries around privately more worry and concern than you might think. The little boy who grew up in a town whose name means "gentle" was given a very similar gift by the God who called him here.

The lesson from Ezekiel for this afternoon describes a stream that begins in the temple, goes out the front door, and eventually nourishes an entire community. There's a lot of measuring of water depth in this lesson. I chose it for Ken not only because he too had to do a lot of precise measuring in his work, but also because he was a man of great depth who asked a lot of good questions about life and its meaning. He was interested in what it meant to lead a good life, a moral life. He wondered regularly if he was pleasing God.

Sometimes religion can get bogged down in little inconsequential stuff and silly arguments that don't matter a whole lot. Those were not Ken's concerns. He read widely. He cared about poor people and how national decisions impacted the poor. He wondered about creation and its origins and whether he had been a good man.

In short, there was a live connection for Ken between church and street, church and this community. Just as the healing water from the temple in Ezekiel's vision brought life wherever it went, so too was Ken's baptism into Christ the defining identity for his public life in this community. Baptism for Ken wasn't just some theological ticket you get punched for the next life. Instead, baptism had everything to do with this life.

His life as a pharmacist, a husband, a dad, a friend — all filtered through this watery identity of grace as a child of God called to serve in Walhalla, South Carolina. It's a heck of a promise Ezekiel makes: "Everything will live where the river goes." It was this old river, with its source in God, that gave Ken the courage and gumption to be who he was and do what he did. It wasn't just by chance that we were given this man to know and love. God claimed him and poured certain gifts into him. This man who grew up in a town called "gentle."

Writing the sermon will help the preacher gain access to a listener's imagination in ways that didactic discourse cannot.

Gaining access to a listener's imagination will require artful and measured language—partly because few outsiders are consciously invited into such a private place, and partly because a lot is going on (much of it rather dark) in the recesses of anyone's cluttered mind.

I was prowling around in the Apocrypha recently and ran across a rather bizarre tale in 4 Maccabees. The book features the tyrant Antiochus Epiphanes, who is trying to blot out Jewish traditions and make everyone come around to the Greek way of life. In one section of the book, Antiochus threatens to torture seven Jewish brothers unless they renounce the tradition and eat the flesh of swine.

> When he had said these things, he ordered the instruments of torture to be brought forward so as to persuade them out of fear to eat the defiling food. When the guards had placed before them wheels and joint-dislocators, rack and hooks and catapults and cauldrons, braziers and thumbscrews and iron claws and wedges and bellows, the tyrant resumed speaking: "Be afraid, young fellows, whatever justice you revere will be merciful to you when you transgress under compulsion." (4 Macc. 8:12–14)

All seven brothers in turn, with their mom cheering them on, refuse to transgress and eat the tyrant's pork chops and bacon; as a consequence, they endure awful acts of brutality and torture that I won't go into here. These stories of culinary bravery were no doubt told around campfire and hearth, certainly heard by Jesus as a child when others recalled heroes of the faith.

When Jesus basically dismissed the whole dietary system (Mark 7), it was a lot to take. If you were going to build a case against Jesus, compile a compendium of sayings (the top ten) that really ticked people off, you couldn't do any better than this outrageous maxim: "There is nothing outside a person that by going in can defile, but the things that come out are what defile" (Mark 7:15).

Jesus is after our hearts, what's rolling around unfiltered in the human imagination. "This people honors me with their lips, but their hearts are far from me" (Mark 7:6, quoting Isaiah). How does Jesus get at my heart, the locus where my real and true self resides? The rather dark terrain of the inner life that ultimately shapes much of my good and bad behavior?

The people that heard Jesus's words were used to measuring righteousness from the outside in, certainly revering the bravery of the Maccabean brothers. Avoid certain foods, certain animals, certain people, certain words—a handy checklist of taboos and no-no's—and you were home free with God. (Many modern Christians still use this checklist system.) People certainly became irked with Jesus because he fiddled around with a centuries-old system of measuring righteousness. But they were also uncomfortable with the man because his mode of teaching and preaching gained regular access to the very complicated inner life of his listeners. Frederick Buechner writes,

> So if preachers or lecturers are to say anything that really matters to anyone including themselves, they must say it not just to the public part of us that considers interesting thoughts about the gospel and how to preach it, but to the private, inner part too, to the part of us all where our dreams come from, both our good dreams and our bad dreams.[11]

Regularly reading poets and novelists (writers whose livelihood depends upon gaining access to a reader's imagination) can shape a preacher's rhetorical strategies and language choices.[12] After I graduated from seminary, reading excellent fiction helped my preaching more than most anything else I could name. So find time to read good writers.

In one of his books, Eugene Peterson describes how he penciled the initials "F.D." into his appointment calendar at the same time each week. He got through a large chunk of the writings of Fyodor Dostoevsky in this fashion over the course of several years. Regular reading doesn't magically insure effective preaching, but I cannot think of an effective preacher who isn't also a faithful reader.

Get It All Out: The First Draft

If we assume that all effective preaching is Spirit-inspired, it perhaps goes without saying that the first draft of your sermon will be rather messy and unruly, certainly not ready to preach the moment after the Friday morning pastor-writer spills it all out on paper. The Holy Spirit at Pentecost knocked over tables with a powerful wind and set timid disciples aflame and into the same streets that left them scampering into the shadows fifty days before. There is certainly a time for such unedited and untethered sermons after a preacher gains the trust of a congregation willing (over time) to follow their pastor into daring homiletical forays, but most parishes of my acquaintance will not tolerate such fiery (and sometimes unfocused) proclamation on a regular basis.

As you may have noticed in my sermon in Chapter Four, I once used the following phrase and immediately regretted it: "Jesus's words that day must have sounded like a loud fart at a funeral." An older and rather refined woman, someone I admire, winced when those words reached her place in the pew. Others laughed, of course, but I lost that one listener for the duration of the sermon. That offending word is rather mild in today's evocative parlance and perhaps used by the woman herself in private. But she (and I daresay others) weren't quite ready for its introduction into a cherished worship space. Similarly, a friend once told me of an illustration he used involving an incident that occurred during his morning shower, which only served to lead a few listeners to the unintended imagery of their pastor without an alb and wearing nothing else.

When a preacher uses certain images, they can distract a listener or lead to rather dark rabbit holes. Faithful commitment to editing offers the grace of "second thoughts" applied to initially perceived cleverness concerning things like bodily functions and other unhelpful images of the pastor best left on the cutting-room floor. Even so, the first draft is a time to get everything out on paper without worrying about how your words might be perceived. Anne Lamott writes,

> A friend of mine says that the first draft is the down draft—you just get it down. The second draft is the up draft—you fix it up. You try to say what you have to say more accurately. And the third draft is the dental draft, where you check every tooth, to see if it is loose or cramped or decayed, or even, God help us, healthy.[13]

I've found that oral editing (going paragraph by paragraph at the keyboard) to be a helpful method of cutting words from the sermon that don't sound quite right or may not be germane to the main theme (more on this in the next chapter). If a sentence of your sermon draft is difficult for you to read aloud on the page, then there's a very high likelihood that it will be difficult to understand in the pew. If something doesn't sound quite right at your writing desk, the context of Sunday morning won't mysteriously correct the problem. Use Friday to polish the draft. I typically read the draft aloud three times (with changes made during each oral reading) before setting it aside for the morning. Oral editing will also help familiarize the preacher with the sermon to a point that reliance on the actual manuscript in the pulpit will be minimized.

Address Congregational Context

In summary, developing a discipline for the weekly writing of sermons will inevitably help a new pastor carefully address various parish issues that will naturally find steady exposure in the regular rhythms of the church year through the power of the three-year lectionary cycle. Church leaders will want to know a pastor's opinion on pressing challenges facing the congregation. That's part of why they called you as an ordained leader. But even more than your opinion concerning how change might occur, the lasting wisdom of Jesus and the prophets must hold sway. The ultimate litmus test for any congregation is not whether a certain body of people is "successful" in a certain context (often measured, regrettably, via attendance and offerings), but instead whether those assembled around word and sacrament have been faithful in listening to a Lord speaking in the present through a very old tradition and its ancient texts. There are no shortcuts to such faithful listening. We follow a man who said, "For the gate is narrow and the road is hard that leads to life, and there are few who find it" (Matt. 7:14).

Parishioners may not agree with everything their minister offers from the pulpit, but creative disagreement can be healthy as long as conflict over parish direction and purpose is centered in the words of Jesus rather than the opinions of the pastor. Sometimes a large percentage of the congregation awaits conversion to Christ, a process that is always unfinished. Whether listeners choose to follow Christ should never be confused with the faithful sounding of Christ's call by the congregation's leadership.

Sermons faithfully prepared and delivered can change an unhealthy congregation. Sermons invite willing listeners to fall in love with God's life-changing Word and the ways of the church's Lord revealed therein. This will take time and pastoral patience with predictable resistance. Jesus, please recall, wasn't immediately embraced by his listeners.

Like any good teacher, a preacher will use the sermon to invite people to adopt some of the same disciplines now hopefully in view and discerned in their pastor from the pulpit on Sunday morning. In the process of writing sermons involving prayer, listening, testimony, and portable recitation of texts in a variety of settings, pastors are modeling faithful discipleship for the congregation.

7
SATURDAY

Rehearsing

Practice Your Pronunciation

There are important differences between writing a sermon and delivering one. I heard a community Thanksgiving sermon a few years ago where the preacher was using a perfectly acceptable illustration based upon the behavior of the dog Snoopy in one of the classic comic strips by Charles M. Schulz. The problem centered upon pronunciation. Instead of clearly saying the phrase "Peanuts strip," the words of the preacher came out "penis strip" at least three times. I'm sure that the congregation understood the preacher's intent, given the overall context featuring an amusing beagle dog, but I asked good friends afterwards if they heard what I just heard, and they all agreed.

Many years ago in rural South Carolina, I listened to a preacher describe his failed (novice) attempt to milk a cow. The illustration fit the sermon's theme and aim, but the pastor got stuck on describing how he tried to engage the cow's udders. He then proceeded to try and pronounce the word "teat," rummaging back and forth between "tit" and "teet," repeatedly and embarrassingly. I looked around the congregation. Several teenagers had to rise and leave the room to keep from laughing.

All preachers mispronounce some words. I somehow grew up pronouncing Chihuahua as "Chihooa-hooa" on the printed page even though I named the diminutive canine correctly when I saw one. The word "ethereal" still trips me up because I tend to incorrectly stress the last syllable using the word "real."

Poor pronunciation and delivery can sink a sermon or lead listeners to places in the imagination that are unintended and preventable. I'm not talking about regional accent here. As a Southerner, for example, I love the various geographical lilts, and I would never encourage a beginning preacher to lose a distinctive brogue. Still, sermon rehearsal—listening to your proclamation privately, perhaps with the assistance of a recording device, or in front of a trusted friend—can literally save a sermon from the derailment experienced by all pastors on occasion as a result of haphazard oral preparation and poor word choice.

Jesus did indeed advise his followers to "not worry about . . . what you are to say; for the Holy Spirit will teach you at that very hour what you ought to say" (Luke 12:11–12). But please recall that the "very hour" described here isn't the worship hour (preaching) but rather a testimonial defense involving persecution and suggesting clear urgency. My pastoral assumption, thirty years out of seminary, is that "persecution" in various forms will indeed haunt pastors who cut corners with sermon preparation.

Preaching effective sermons still rates very high (ecumenically) in terms of pastoral expectations from parish call committees. Like it or not, Sunday visitors and newcomers to church life often make affiliation judgments based upon how a pastor comes across during the sermon. Barbara Brown Taylor said somewhere that she was grateful for weekly Eucharist in the Episcopal tradition, especially when her sermon failed on a particular Sunday. But there are still few moments in a congregation's public ministry more scrutinized with expectation than the Sunday sermon. It behooves pastors to prepare faithfully.

Edit and Revise

Fiction writer Benjamin Percy likens the editing process to his family's purchase of an old house described this way by their realtor: "It's got good bones." The structure of the house was basically sound and strong, but practically every room needed attention, requiring either painting, new light fixtures, or, in some instances, a wall that needed shoring up or even replacing. Some parts of the house could be torn out and used elsewhere.

Percy admits that revision of one's writing is difficult even when necessary. "That is why I used to resist it. When I received comments on my work, my eyes skimmed over the criticism and honed in on the compliments. That is no way to be."[1]

Pastors aren't usually blessed with a helpful professional editor before submitting work for the public eye (and ear). Major differences exist between writing fiction and writing a sermon. But Percy's observation about the "bones" of his writing strikes home with me. There are components of any sermon that can profitably be moved around, amended, or deleted altogether, perhaps awaiting use in the future. (Fred Craddock was a proponent of saving all sermon notes on a particular sermon for possible use in a future sermon on the same texts three years hence.)

Ezekiel's famous vision of the Valley of Dry Bones (37:1–14) fits well here. Ultimately, it is the vivifying breath of the Spirit that brings life and flesh to bones in the middle of the valley. The bones themselves weren't valueless, completely displaced from tradition and God's power. But something more was needed to bring the bones back to life.

Similarly, Saturday's work on the sermon (this can be brief; Saturday was my "play" day with our kids) revisits your work that has been gestating since Friday's morning time at your writing desk. Even Jesus's bones needed "time in the tomb" prior to resurrection. Consider this time in your sermon preparation process something of a Holy Saturday in a homiletical Triduum.

8
SUNDAY

Offering

Observe Liturgical Silence[1]

Consider: that short silence observed most weeks during the confession at the beginning of the service. We'll belt out something mostly in-tune momentarily, but first address a God "to whom all desires are known and from whom no secrets are hid." *All desires. No secrets.* Couldn't we keep a few?

The confessional silence only lasts about thirty seconds or so before an absolution. But I've been lingering in the silence lately, pondering the volume and variety of flaws and foibles that surely follow us all into worship and never get confessed (specifically) aloud—an overwhelming thought if considered for very long.

Lutherans have a private rite of "Individual Confession and Forgiveness" that includes anointing with oil, a rite used sparingly by penitents in my three decades as a pastor. I wonder what Sunday morning would sound like if we came clean and confessed all of it out loud simultaneously—an intriguing confessional *glossolalia* that might increase church attendance.

Early in the book of Acts, Peter rises for the equivalent of the Sunday-morning announcement period (1:15–19). Due to a lack of punctuation in the original Greek, graphic information about Judas's demise is either rendered *aloud* to all gathered or rendered *parenthetically* to the reader, depending on the chosen English Bible version. I'm intrigued by the older Revised Standard Version (RSV), where Peter announces the nitty-gritty for all in attendance: "Falling headlong, he burst open in the middle and all his bowels gushed out." Such detail surely awakened any dozing worshipers, but I can't imagine such an announcement in any congregation I've ever served.

Most Sunday announcements are usually rather sanitized. Joe's upcoming back surgery. The passing of Sally's grandmother. The softball game at seven. Important concerns, to be sure, but any attentive congregant will notice how some parish news is publicly reported, and other events are only whispered about. In any congregation a line of propriety exists that pastors usually dare not cross, so we keep items politely acceptable for Sunday-morning sensibilities. But who decides where the line is drawn? Perhaps we save the really scandalous stuff for private reflection in those thirty seconds.

I've come to value these silent ticks and tocks in liturgical time like few other moments, and I suspect it is the relevance and immediacy of this half-minute that has prompted many to get out of bed to kneel in the first place, searching for how one can indeed go on after costly mistakes. If this is true, I'm wondering if it is the church's neglect of our common condition (happy bromides on a happy Sunday morning with lots of exclamation points) that eventually sends many toward the exits, looking elsewhere for meaning, a chance for repentance, and grace.

Perhaps pastors should halt the service (full stop) just after the absolution and ask out loud, "Does anyone realize what just happened here? Your sins and mine—including our whispered secrets and unhealthy desires—have been heard, truly heard, and audaciously forgiven."

A lot is going on during liturgical silences, including the built-in silence (in the Lutheran tradition) following the sermon. Don't rush through moments after the sermon with words like, "Let's now all rise for Hymn 237."

Avoid Theatrics

A variety of emotions, actions, theological history, and congregational memory comprise the Sunday-morning liturgy, literally "the work of the people" and not the work solely of a pastor.

It's tempting to view worship similarly to theatre, with an audience that assembles regularly to watch certain actors perform components of a set script that may change slightly with the season. An organist leads the hymns. A soloist rises and sits. Offering plates are passed around in measured coordination. A pastor talks about Jesus. Bread and wine are ingested. And those in the pew may be moved, angered, or bored by those performing up front and "onstage" on a weekly basis. We all go home until next Sunday's performance.

But in worship, the notion of audience/stage shifts dramatically when a congregation realizes that they are full participants and actors in an ongoing drama, not just onlookers watching the drama from a distance. (I think it was Søren Kierkegaard who noted that the only real audience in worship is God.)

I recently read *Elmer Gantry* for the first time, Sinclair Lewis's classic novel published in 1927. The story centers upon a rather shifty pastor whose pulpit tirades against local vice serve to draw large crowds to watch accusations and antics that are carefully staged and later reviewed in local newspapers. Everything in worship leads up to the drama of the sermon and Gantry's large ego, massaged by masses who are basically there to see what outrageous thing he'll say next.

In the novel Lewis takes time to describe several different pastors in the fictional Midwestern city of Zenith. Frank Stallard, one of Elmer's seminary classmates, can see right through the pulpit theatrics of his old friend, but seems to be losing his passion for parish ministry entirely:

> Of what value were doggerel hymns raggedly sung? What value in sermons, when the congregation seemed not at all different from people who never heard sermons? Were all ministers and all churches, Frank wondered, merely superstitious survivals, merely fire-insurance? Suppose there were such things as inspiring sermons. Suppose there could be such a curious office as minister, as Professional Good Man; such a thing as learning Goodness just as one learned plumbing or dentistry. Even so, what training had he or his classmates, or his professors—whose D.D. degrees did not protect them from indigestion and bad tempers—in this trade of Professional Goodness?[2]

By the story's conclusion, Lewis (who attended many Sunday worship services in researching the novel) seems to have no sympathy at all for most expressions of American Christianity. This classic study of hypocrisy in church life in the first quarter of the twentieth century brought threats of physical violence to the author and even suggestions for his imprisonment. But the questions Lewis places within the imagination of Pastor Stallard seemed to me eerily prescient for many recent seminary graduates serving churches a century later.

What is a pastor's primary role in congregational life? A professional do-gooder, cajoling parishioners into proper behavior and unmistakable virtue, especially with the weekly leverage of the sermon, when people sit passively as captive listeners? Reading the novel caused me once again to ponder the purpose of the sermon in the worship setting and preaching's role in the ongoing sanctification and spiritual growth of regular listeners.

Reframe Preaching as Offering

"I appeal to you therefore, brothers and sisters, by the mercies of God, to present your bodies as a living sacrifice, holy and acceptable to God, which is your spiritual worship" (Rom. 12:1).

The familiar adverb "therefore" in this verse is a deceptively complex word in that it refers back to the previous eleven chapters in Romans where Saint Paul makes powerful and theologically complex arguments concerning our justification (3:28); baptismal death in Christ (6:1–11); our inability to save ourselves (7:14–25); and new life in the Spirit (8:1–39). As Christians we risk offering our "bodies as a living sacrifice" not to get God to love us any more than we are currently loved, but because the offering now springs from the theological truth that we have already died in baptism and can radically offer our lives back to the God who birthed us newly. We have died to self-improvement, merit-based reward, and fear of death itself. We slowly loosen our cautious grip on the things that were paralyzing us. This is the joy of worship, a story cyclically retold through the power of the church year. We offer our bodies on an altar "as a living sacrifice" because Christ has led the way. We make the sign of the cross (Luther's favorite liturgical gesture) as a reminder that in baptism we have been liberated—from death and for ministry—to now live sacrificially and without fear.

"It will not be like the covenant that I made with their ancestors when I took them by the hand to bring them out of the land of Egypt" (Jer. 31:32). Pastors don't have to look back very far in any family picture album in the parish to find snapshots of parents holding their children's hands as they took their first steps out into the world to go somewhere.

Here's a photo on the first day of kindergarten. Five little fingers buried in a much bigger hand, the child not so sure about this new world called "school." And here's another at the beach when the child discovers the joy and the terror of waves for the first time, his little hand latched onto his father's hand as if it's a lifeline. But look at the albums closely. At some point, the hand-holding stopped.

God was the ultimate hand-holder, fretting over his children and getting furious when they didn't comply with his wishes. In fact, much of the first half of the Bible is a series of family snapshots of God trying over and over again to take the hand of his children, with those same kids rebelling and disappointing him. "After all I've done for you," God seems to say.

But then God tries a new approach—a remarkably new approach. Jeremiah calls it a new covenant. "It will not be like the time I held my children by the hand to bring them out of Egypt." This is a rather odd thing for God to say, if you think about it, because the words suggest that even God the Almighty One seems to learn a thing or two in the Bible, and here he learns this: *that love cannot be legislated or coerced.* Only offered.

So, God withdrew his hand and his constant nit-picking over his children's mistakes. He gave his children the wonderful and terrifying gift of freedom. He set them free to make choices. Free to make decisions. Free to forget God or take God for granted; even free to renounce God. In this new covenant, God no longer takes his children by the hand. This freedom is probably both the best *and* the most terrifying gift any of us has ever received.

The freedom to now radically offer one's life in sacrificial response is at the heart of the liturgy, and in the heart of preaching. All authentic preaching is a response to what God has done and what God is doing in Jesus Christ.

Preaching will therefore have an elliptical feel to be completed in the hearts and minds of the listeners. The preacher cannot take a worshiper by the hand (any more than God can) and tie everything up in a little package with a neat bow. Preaching is an offering rooted in the offering of Christ, in turn inviting an offering from those who listen and ponder in the silence that brought them to worship in the first place.

Expect Occasional Sermonic Rejection

There will be Sundays when your sermon will fall flat. And Sundays when your sermon elicits downright anger.

Some sermons just never seem to get off the ground. You feel it during delivery, and the congregation senses your own unfocused circling of the text. It's okay; give yourself a break. Hectic weeks inevitably intrude upon sermon preparation time. And sometimes a pastor isn't able to discern the prodding of the Spirit no matter how much time he or she devotes to preaching disciplines. This is simply the truth: some sermons will bomb. Save them in a file and go back and have a good laugh down the way. The congregation has undoubtedly listened patiently to uninspiring sermons before.

The response of anger is another matter. Some sermons will elicit specific parishioner ire. It's rare that the entire congregation will rise in unison and have the pastor for lunch, so to speak.[3] But negative feedback from individuals should be expected and isn't usually a sign for great alarm.

An angry response, please note, sometimes has nothing to do with the sermon at all. The pastor is a convenient outlet at the door for an unnamed issue that may have been set off internally by an image or a remark from the sermon. This response gives the pastor an opportunity to follow up (with patience and courage) and try to discover what's really bothering the person.

But there will be other times when sermons, faithfully offered and biblically centered, will elicit anger and downright animosity. Parishioners (including their pastor) are often complex people with a variety of hidden biases and unexplored prejudices. Jesus surely receives me "Just as I Am." The Lord just refuses to leave me that way.

Ongoing conversion to Christ is often uncomfortable and even painful because we're leaving one way of living for another. In baptism, the "old Adam" drowns. I can't recall who said he's still a pretty good swimmer. We're quite capable of resistance to change in Christ because much is at stake. Anger is sometimes an authentic response to the change Christ has in mind. Again, Martin Luther likened some forms of preaching to surgery: even when it's needed, few honest people are eager to sign up for it voluntarily.

I recall a woman (and a very faithful person) in one of my parishes who made a beeline for my post-worship greeting post, impatiently breaking through the line to state her case. This was in autumn of 2001, just after the events of 9/11, on All Saints Sunday. The assigned Gospel text was Luke 6:20–31, the more pointed version of the Beatitudes. Jesus's challenging words there include an imperative to "Love your enemies, do good to those who hate you, bless those who curse you, pray for those who abuse you" (6:27–28).

In the sermon, I'd encouraged the congregation to audaciously pray for Osama bin Laden, with the assumption that if anyone could change the misguided man, God could. I don't recall her exact words, but this faithful woman was furious with me for encouraging such a thing. I listened to her for a while and eventually suggested she might be more appropriately mad at Jesus. These were his words, not mine. She didn't like that, either.

I'll say it again. To attempt to live by the words of Jesus will be painful at times. His words regularly raised the ire of religious people in the century in which they were first spoken. And they will often do the same in the twenty-first. It's worth citing again: "Woe to you when all speak well of you,"

Jesus says in this same section from Luke (6:26). There will be Sundays when parishioners won't be happy with their pastor for bringing an uncomfortable word.

One ongoing pastoral task is to help a congregation come to terms with the word "Lord." Our first and primary allegiance is offered to Jesus, regardless of risk or cost. Christians have a single Lord. Americans live in a current climate where political expediency can sometimes unconsciously supersede this primary allegiance. Lectionary preaching will (over time) serve to reorient a congregation to a voice more important than any president or any authority. There is a pastoral art to clearly preaching his gospel words in an era of fake news, lies, and political deception.[4]

Don't take it personally. You're probably on the right track when people get mad. In actuality, they're often angry at Jesus. A pastor is his proximate spokesperson.

Become Both Friend and Strange

A pastor needs friends. When I was in seminary, a debate raged over whether a pastor could have close friendships with members of the congregation. The dangers were obvious, among them the difficulty of speaking a truthful and perhaps prophetic word to someone with whom a pastor had become close, socially.

Largely missing in the debate was the general need for friendship in a vocation that requires confidentiality, includes regular stress, and offers the potentially isolating reality of daring to speak for God to the community. My wife, Cindy, and I (and our three children) have had several close friendships down through the years with church members in four different parish settings. It was understood that conversation about sensitive church matters was off-limits, and clear that after departing a certain parish I couldn't be called back to do "special" weddings and funerals, even privately. This is sometimes harder to maintain than one might think, but certainly possible. Church members need to see their pastor as a human being who laughs, cries, and doubts like any other friend.

With that said, there will always be a part of the pastoral vocation that suggests a bit of distance, requiring the counsel and collaboration of other clergy. Even in small rural settings where meetings with another pastor in your denomination may not be practically feasible, ecumenical pastoral friendships will surely exist. Don't attempt pastoral ministry for the long haul solo. It's often a weird life with a variety of rather toxic situations and puzzling challenges with no initially easy outcomes.

As one stands between God and people in preaching, a received word from the Holy Spirit is fundamentally odd. If Jesus "is the reflection of God's glory and the exact imprint of God's very being, and he sustains all things by his powerful word" (Heb. 1:3), then those called to lead his church will also be a bit different and strange, seeing life and the world angularly over a career involving the weekly preparation of faithful sermons. If the feeling of strangeness is absent, perhaps a pastor has taken one too many shortcuts.

C. H. Spurgeon (1834–1892), who preached in London for thirty-eight years, once said: "I have tried, especially of late, to take no more notice of man's praise than his blame."[5] Spurgeon's striving is admittedly difficult and sometimes isolating, but an important consideration because a pastor ultimately serves Christ and the apostolic tradition rather than a specific congregation. Pastors sign on for a career of feeling a little out of sync with the good people we are called to lead.

Perhaps the idea of pastor as "stranger" should be replaced with the idea of pastor as simply strange. There is one Jewish tradition where the priest called to go before God in the Holy of Holies made sure to tie a rope around one ankle so that friends could haul him out to safety if the encounter with the divine was just too much. Moses usually appeared veiled before God for good reason.

Sunday's service concludes. You've greeted a long line of worshipers. Sit in an empty pew for a while and pray. Offer God thanks for the insights punctuating the day's liturgy. Tomorrow will begin the process toward another sermon.

Go in peace. Develop friendships. Embrace your relative oddness.

Epilogue

I was just about to board my bicycle in our garage the other day when I noticed a small box titled "Calendars" at eye level on a shelf. With my bike helmet on (perhaps for added security and safety for this unplanned encounter!), I lifted the lid and saw thirty-one small (3 x 5 inch) red annual pocket calendars. Lutheran pastors used to receive gratis a calendar each December from our denominational publication house. They now charge nominally for "the little red book," and I gladly paid the fee toward the end of my career because there was something about the tactile feel of a real calendar in the pastoral pocket that electronic versions couldn't match.

It was a rather surreal moment, staring at over three decades of cumulative history in one small box—all the meetings, counseling sessions, funerals, classes, weddings, baptisms, hospital calls, living-room chats, parish events, and vacations. It reminded me of the many people a pastor encounters, and the dates and times, and the months passing in a variety of joyful and agonizing moments. I picked up a couple of the calendars and flipped through them, wondering what I could possibly have meant by a rather cryptic entry on a date in March of 1991. I'm not sure how much time passed in the garage that day. Lots of names and faces—Howard, my funeral home friend; Candy and Sandy, the delightful twins; and even Bruce, the annoying man with his business card full of expertise—swam through my imagination.

Eventually I headed out on the bike. It was a beautiful fall day, and I thought of a prayer I have always liked, "For Those Whose Work Is Invisible," written by novelist Mary Gordon. Arriving home after the bicycle ride, with all the calendar appointments still in mind, I looked it up.

> For those who paint the underside of boats, makers of ornamental drains on roofs too high to be seen; for cobblers who labor over inner soles; for seamstresses who stitch the wrong sides of linings; for scholars whose research leads to no obvious discovery; for dentists who polish each gold surface of the fillings of upper molars; for sewer engineers and those who repair water mains; for electricians. . . . For all those whose work is for Your eye only, who sleep in peace or do not sleep in peace, knowing that their effects are unknown. Protect them from downheartedness and from diseases of the eye. Grant them perseverance, for the sake of Your love which is humble, invisible and heedless of reward.[1]

In this beautiful prayer, she doesn't mention pastors, especially new ones, much of whose work is also invisible at first.

So, I will now.

Notes

Foreword

1. Craig R. Dykstra, "A Way of Seeing: Imagination and the Pastoral Life," *The Christian Century*, April 8, 2008, 29, 31.

2. Wendell Berry, *Jayber Crow* (Washington: Counterpoint, 2000), 161.

3. Giovannino Guareschi, "Shotgun Wedding," chapter 21 in *Little World: Don Camillo and His Flock*, http://www.meaning-of-life.info /DonCamilloandhisFlock21.html.

Introduction

1. Not her real name or home state.

2. Much has been written about this last stressor, largely unknown for most pastors of my generation. (I graduated from seminary in 1985.) Here I will only make the perhaps-obvious observation that school debt not only cripples a pastor's ability to give sacrificially, but also potentially silences a pastor's zeal in preaching prophetically about money.

3. Kathleen Norris, *Amazing Grace: A Vocabulary of Faith* (New York: Riverhead Books, 1998), 67.

4. C. S. Lewis, *The Screwtape Letters* (New York: Bantam Books, 1982), 7. Italics in original.

5. Willimon, Lischer, Long, Taylor, Forbes, and Craddock, to name a few.

6. I am hopeful also that seasoned pastors will benefit from this book, as many of the challenges named in the introduction never completely go away in some locales. Even so, the book's central aim is for the newly ordained.

Chapter 1

1. I met Ernest once, early in my pastoral career, at a preaching conference at Kirkridge Retreat Center in Pennsylvania. Educated at Bob Jones University and Princeton Seminary, Ernest eventually was called to serve Riverside Church in New York City as senior minister. I can think of few preachers in the latter part of the twentieth century who possessed an exposure to such varied theological perspectives. If you can find them, his sermons are a treat.

2. I also recommend using a daily (two-year) lectionary for morning devotional use—especially if your knowledge of the Bible's vast scope upon leaving seminary (like mine at the time) is limited.

3. Burton L. Visotsky, *Reading the Book: Making the Bible a Timeless Text* (New York: Schocken, 1991), 18.

4. Barbara Brown Taylor, *When God Is Silent* (Boston: Cowley Publications, 1998), 85–86. Italics in original.

5. Anne Lamott, *Bird by Bird: Some Instructions on Writing and Life* (New York: Anchor Books, 1994), 18. Lamott's book is an excellent resource for preachers learning to write sermons.

6. Thomas G. Long, "Stolen Goods: Tempted to Plagiarize," *The Christian Century*, April 17, 2007, 21. Long offers a compelling case concerning the damage rendered to both preacher and parishioners from the popular use of online sermons. Although over a decade old, this article is the best I have come across on this topic.

7. I would never trade the gift of lasting inter-generational friendships in the congregations I have served. The lives of younger

adults, apart from church, are often diminished by the lack of friendships with older people who might offer wisdom and guidance in a transient culture. Younger pastors, however, are often called to serve congregations where relationships with peers their own age may be infrequent.

8. In the receiving line after worship, I used to be distressed when someone offered a positive comment about my sermon that was widely divergent from my homiletical intent. I have since concluded that the Holy Spirit is fully aware of what a listener needs to hear and process. See Isaiah 55:8–11.

9. Gertrude Mueller Nelson, *To Dance with God: Family Ritual and Community Celebration* (Mahwah, NJ: Paulist Press, 1986).

10. See Michael Ende, *The Neverending Story*, translated by Ralph Manheim (New York: Doubleday, 1983).

11. I am indebted to New Testament scholar Ched Myers for this insight concerning Mark's conclusion.

Chapter 2

1. This coastal junket is a fair distance from Galilee. The implication may be that he is here at the shore for a short break from the rigors of an increasingly demanding ministry. See Mark 1:36, for example, where Simon and companions "hunt" for Jesus after he tries to withdraw for prayer. The verb here literally suggests tracking down an animal with the intent to catch it. Ever felt such pressure in your ministry?

2. Benjamin Percy, *Thrill Me: Essays on Fiction* (Minneapolis: Graywolf Press, 2016), 119. Italics in original.

3. Andrew Sullivan, "I Used to Be a Human Being," *New York Magazine*, September 18, 2016. This is a long essay, but very worthwhile in its entirety.

4. Anne Lamott, *Bird by Bird: Some Instructions on Writing and Life* (New York: Anchor Books, 1994), 136–37.

5. Cited in William H. Willimon, *Sighing for Eden: Sin, Evil, and the Christian Faith* (Nashville: Abingdon Press, 1985), 24.

6. Diane Ackerman, *A Natural History of the Senses* (New York: Vintage Books, 1990), xv–xvi. Italics in original.

Chapter 3

1. Names of parishioners in this section have been altered.

2. Kurt Andersen, "How America Lost Its Mind," *The Atlantic*, September 2017, 79.

3. Sally A. Brown, "Preaching as Spiritual Formation," *Journal for Preachers* (Lent 1998), 29. Italics in original. Note the year this article was published and the explosion of cyber-misinformation in the twenty years since, underscoring a pastor's counterformational preaching task.

4. "Woe to you when all speak well of you," says Jesus in Luke 6:26. If a pastor is uniformly praised by the congregation, there's a good chance of vocational avoidance.

5. See Frank G. Honeycutt, *Preaching to Skeptics and Seekers* (Nashville: Abingdon Press, 2001).

6. Thomas G. Long, *What Shall We Say? Evil, Suffering, and the Crisis of Faith* (Grand Rapids: Eerdmans, 2011), 114. Italics in original.

7. See Amos 9:7–8, for example.

8. A good Bible dictionary and an analytical concordance are indispensable exegetical tools for a preacher's library.

Chapter 4

1. Harper Lee, *To Kill a Mockingbird* (New York: Grand Central Publishing, 1960), 162.

2. Fred B. Craddock, *Preaching* (Nashville: Abingdon Press, 1985), 25–26.

3. Miriam Toews, *A Complicated Kindness* (Berkeley, CA: Counterpoint Press, 2004), 6.

4. Alice K. Turner, *The History of Hell* (New York: Harcourt, Brace and Company, 1993), 4. Italics in original.

5. Don't miss Karl Malden's classic sermon, "Death Comes Unexpectedly," from the movie *Pollyanna* (1960).

6. Dallas Willard, *The Divine Conspiracy: Rediscovering Our Hidden Life in God* (San Francisco: HarperCollins, 1998), 302.

7. This seems to be one of the conclusions reached in C. S. Lewis's extended parable, *The Great Divorce* (1945), where many who arrive in heaven don't like the place, choosing instead to return to earth.

8. Craddock, *Preaching*, 155–56.

9. Neil Postman, *Amusing Ourselves to Death: Public Discourse in the Age of Show Business* (New York: Penguin Books, 1985), 44.

10. Postman, *Amusing Ourselves to Death*, 44–46.

11. Craig Barnes, "Lessons from the Keller Controversy," *The Christian Century*, August 16, 2017, 35.

12. See especially William H. Willimon, *Pastor: The Theology and Practice of Ordained Ministry* (Nashville: Abingdon Press, 2002), and Eugene H. Peterson, *Working the Angles: The Shape of Pastoral Integrity* (Grand Rapids: Eerdmans, 1989). These two books are indispensable in this regard for recent seminary graduates.

Chapter 5

1. Thomas G. Long, *What Shall We Say? Evil, Suffering, and the Crisis of Faith* (Grand Rapids: Eerdmans, 2011), 130.

2. Ebenezer Lutheran Church (Columbia, SC).

Chapter 6

1. Wendell Berry, "Creation Myth," *A Part* (San Francisco: North Point Press, 1980), 45.

2. Thomas G. Long, *The Witness of Preaching* (Louisville: Westminster John Knox Press, 1989), 183.

3. Benjamin Percy, *Thrill Me: Essays on Fiction* (Minneapolis: Graywolf Press, 2016), 33–34.

4. University Lutheran Church (Clemson, SC).

5. David Sedaris, *Me Talk Pretty One Day* (New York: Little, Brown and Company, 2000), 177, 179.

6. Harry Emerson Fosdick, "What Is the Matter with Preaching?," in *Harry Emerson Fosdick's Art of Preaching: An Anthology*, ed. Lionel Crocker (Springfield, IL: Charles C. Thomas Publisher, 1971), 30.

7. Genesis 32:11.

8. Joseph Heller, *God Knows* (New York: Alfred A. Knopf, 1984), 19.

9. Brian Doyle, *Leaping: Revelations and Epiphanies* (Chicago: Loyola Press, 2013), 62.

10. Richard Lischer, *Stations of the Heart: Parting with a Son* (New York: Alfred A. Knopf, 2013), 220.

11. Frederick Buechner, *Telling the Truth: The Gospel as Tragedy, Comedy, and Fairy Tale* (San Francisco: Harper and Row, 1977), 4.

12. See Cornelius Plantinga Jr., *Reading for Preaching: The Preacher in Conversation with Storytellers, Biographers, Poets, and Journalists* (Grand Rapids: Eerdmans, 2013).

13. Anne Lamott, *Bird by Bird: Some Instructions on Writing and Life* (New York: Anchor Books, 1994), 25–26.

Chapter 7

1. Benjamin Percy, *Thrill Me: Essays on Fiction* (Minneapolis: Graywolf Press, 2016), 163.

Chapter 8

1. The opening section of this chapter (in slightly different form) first appeared in Frank G. Honeycutt, "Thirty Seconds of Silence," *Living Lutheran*, August 2017, 5.

2. Sinclair Lewis, *Elmer Gantry* (New York: The New American Library, 1927), 229.

3. Although do recall Luke 4:29, of course, and my earlier suggestion about researching area topography.

4. For an extended reflection on pastoral truth-telling, see Frank G. Honeycutt, *The Truth Shall Make You Odd: Speaking with Pastoral Integrity in Awkward Situations* (Grand Rapids: Brazos Press, 2011).

5. Cited in William H. Willimon, *Pastor: The Theology and Practice of Ordained Ministry* (Nashville: Abingdon Press, 2003), 97.

Epilogue

1. Mary Gordon, "Prayers," in *The Best Spiritual Writing 2000*, ed. Philip Zaleski (San Francisco: HarperCollins, 2000), 143–44.

Bibliography

Ackerman, Diane. *A Natural History of the Senses.* New York: Vintage Books, 1990.

Andersen, Kurt. "How America Lost Its Mind." *The Atlantic,* September 2017, 76–91.

Barnes, Craig. "Lessons from the Keller Controversy." *The Christian Century,* August 16, 2017, 35.

Berry, Wendell. "Creation Myth." Page 45 in *A Part.* San Francisco: North Point Press, 1980.

Brown, Sally A. "Preaching as Spiritual Formation." *Journal for Preachers,* Lent 1998.

Buechner, Frederick. *Telling the Truth: The Gospel as Tragedy, Comedy, and Fairy Tale.* San Francisco: Harper and Row, 1977.

Craddock, Fred B. *Preaching.* Nashville: Abingdon Press, 1985.

Doyle, Brian. *Leaping: Revelations and Epiphanies.* Chicago: Loyola Press, 2013.

Ende, Michael. *The Neverending Story.* Translated by Ralph Manheim. New York: Doubleday, 1983.

Fosdick, Harry Emerson. "What Is the Matter with Preaching?" *Harper's Magazine,* July 1928, 133–41. Also available in *Harry*

Emerson Fosdick's Art of Preaching: An Anthology. Edited by Lionel Crocker. Springfield, IL: Charles C. Thomas Publisher, 1971.

Gordon, Mary. "Prayers." *Paris Review* 151 (Summer 1999). Also available in *The Best Spiritual Writing 2000*. Edited by Philip Zaleski. San Francisco: HarperCollins, 2000.

Heller, Joseph. *God Knows*. New York: Alfred A. Knopf, 1984.

Honeycutt, Frank G. *Preaching to Skeptics and Seekers*. Nashville: Abingdon Press, 2001.

————. "Thirty Seconds of Silence." *Living Lutheran*, August 2017, 5.

————. *The Truth Shall Make You Odd: Speaking with Pastoral Integrity in Awkward Situations*. Grand Rapids: Brazos Press, 2011.

Lamott, Anne. *Bird by Bird: Some Instructions on Writing and Life*. New York: Anchor Books, 1994.

Lee, Harper. *To Kill a Mockingbird*. New York: Grand Central Publishing, 1960.

Lewis, C. S. *The Great Divorce*. London: Collins, 1946.

————. *The Screwtape Letters*. London: Collins, 1942.

Lewis, Sinclair. *Elmer Gantry*. New York: The New American Library, 1927.

Lischer, Richard. *Stations of the Heart: Parting with a Son*. New York: Alfred A. Knopf, 2013.

Long, Thomas G. "Stolen Goods: Tempted to Plagiarize." *The Christian Century*, April 17, 2007.

————. *What Shall We Say? Evil, Suffering, and the Crisis of Faith*. Grand Rapids: Eerdmans, 2011.

————. *The Witness of Preaching*. Louisville: Westminster John Knox Press, 1989.

Nelson, Gertrude Mueller. *To Dance with God: Family Ritual and Community Celebration*. Mahwah, NJ: Paulist Press, 1986.

Norris, Kathleen. *Amazing Grace: A Vocabulary of Faith*. New York: Riverhead Books, 1998.

Percy, Benjamin. *Thrill Me: Essays on Fiction*. Minneapolis: Graywolf Press, 2016.

Peterson, Eugene H. *Working the Angles: The Shape of Pastoral Integrity*. Grand Rapids: Eerdmans, 1989.

Plantinga, Cornelius, Jr. *Reading for Preaching: The Preacher in Conversation with Storytellers, Biographers, Poets, and Journalists*. Grand Rapids: Eerdmans, 2013.

Pollyanna. Directed by David Swift. Walt Disney Productions, 1960.

Postman, Neil. *Amusing Ourselves to Death: Public Discourse in the Age of Show Business*. New York: Penguin Books, 1985.

Sedaris, David. *Me Talk Pretty One Day*. New York: Little, Brown and Company, 2000.

Sullivan, Andrew. "I Used to Be a Human Being." *New York Magazine*, September 18, 2016.

Taylor, Barbara Brown. *When God Is Silent*. Boston: Cowley Publications, 1998.

Toews, Miriam. *A Complicated Kindness*. Berkeley, CA: Counterpoint Press, 2004.

Turner, Alice K. *The History of Hell*. New York: Harcourt, Brace and Company, 1993.

Visotsky, Burton L. *Reading the Book: Making the Bible a Timeless Text*. New York: Schocken, 1991.

Willard, Dallas. *The Divine Conspiracy: Rediscovering Our Hidden Life in God*. San Francisco: HarperCollins, 1998.

Willimon, William H. *Pastor: The Theology and Practice of Ordained Ministry*. Nashville: Abingdon Press, 2002.

————. *Sighing for Eden: Sin, Evil, and the Christian Faith*. Nashville: Abingdon Press, 1985.